2020/11
OK.

KT-430-997

Get **more** out of libraries

Please return or renew this item by the last date shown.
You can renew online at www.hants.gov.uk/library
Or by phoning 0845 603 5631

Hampshire
County Council

Hampshire
County Council

06/06

CL14 2/03 20k

THE SUNDAY TIMES

C R E A T I N G   S U C C E S S

Understanding
Brands

Peter Cheverton

KOGAN
PAGE

London and Philadelphia

Publisher's note

Every possible effort has been made to ensure that the information contained in this book is accurate at the time of going to press, and the publishers and author cannot accept responsibility for any errors or omissions, however caused. No responsibility for loss or damage occasioned to any person acting, or refraining from action, as a result of the material in this publication can be accepted by the editor, the publisher or the author.

First published in Great Britain in 2002 by Kogan Page Limited as *If You're So Brilliant... How Come Your Brand Isn't Working Hard Enough?*
Reissued in 2005 as *How Come Your Brand Isn't Working Hard Enough?*
This edition published in 2006 as *Understanding Brands*

120 Pentonville Road
London N1 9JN
United Kingdom
www.kogan-page.co.uk

525 South 4th Street, #241
Philadelphia PA 19147
USA

ISBN 0 7494 4665 X

British Library Cataloguing-in-Publication Data

A CIP record for this book is available from the British Library.

Library of Congress Cataloging-in-Publication Data

Cheverton, Peter.
  Understanding brands / Peter Cheverton.
    p. cm. -- (Creating success)
  "First published in Great Britain in 2002 by Kogan Page Limited as If you're so brilliant, how come your brand isn't working hard enough? Reissued in 2005 as How come your brand isn't working hard enough?"
  ISBN 0-7494-4665-X
  1. Brand name products. 2. Product management. I. Cheverton, Peter. How Come Your Brand Isn't Working Hard Enough? II. Title. III. Series.
  HD69.B7U53 2006
  658.8'27--dc22
                        2006008964

Typeset by Saxon Graphics Ltd, Derby
Printed and bound in the United Kingdom by Bell & Bain, Glasgow

Contents

Preface

Getting your brand to work harder, to ensure that it makes its proper mark, isn't just about money. Indeed, money may be the least of your problems. Getting brands to work on small budgets is more than possible; it is the norm. Hearing a professor of marketing say that branding was a waste of time unless you had £10 million to spend was one of the impulses behind the writing of this book.

Good branding takes a lot of good thinking. This is not to say that brands should be managed by intellectuals, or that we should allow the jargon-spouting folk from 'the agency' to take hold of the reins. Brand management certainly engages the brain but it doesn't disengage common sense, nor should it stop us from using everyday language. The fact that too many books on branding read like PhD theses on anthropology was another of the impulses behind the writing of this rather more practically minded book.

This book is intended for the business manager, the marketer, the brand manager, and all those involved with building and defining their own brands. So many branding books appear designed for the professional advertising executive and associated media and design folk, that I have deliberately steered a course towards the *owners* of the brand rather than the agencies that will support them.

Some people argue that brands are dying, others that they are the cornerstone of our civilisation, and yet others see them as a curse of modern life. What we can agree is that brands are changing, as they always have and always must to survive. In this, brands inhabit a brutally Darwinian world, and the key question for those wishing to survive must be – what is meant by 'the fittest'? In answering this question I have tried to navigate a course between the lovers and the haters of brands, occasionally flirting with each camp as seems appropriate.

Above all else, the brand is something to be managed; it must be protected, nurtured, exploited and changed. Few marketers will have the task of creating a brand from scratch, most will inherit one, for better or worse. Inheriting a brand is like inheriting a grand stately home – a significant luxury, a major responsibility, and occasionally an impending liability. Helping you to achieve good brand management is the purpose of this book.

Part I

Defining the brand – its purpose and its benefits

A good brand will make you feel good about the choice you have made, to buy it and to use it. A good brand will help you make that choice in the first place, and it can do that because it knows how to make you feel good. The good brand, as illustrated in Figure PI.1 (see page 2), is a virtuous circle of action and reaction, give and take.

That it can do all these things shows what a complex thing a brand is. Much more than a name and a slogan, and substantially more than an advertisement – these things are but window dressing compared to the heart of a brand. The heart of the brand is an idea, and ideas can change, and be changed – that's how a brand lives, learns and grows.

A name, however great it sounds round the agency board-room table, backed by a £2 million advertising campaign, but without the injection of an idea, is not a brand – it's a heavily promoted name. This book aims to help you find the idea within your brand, its definition, its identity, its soul.

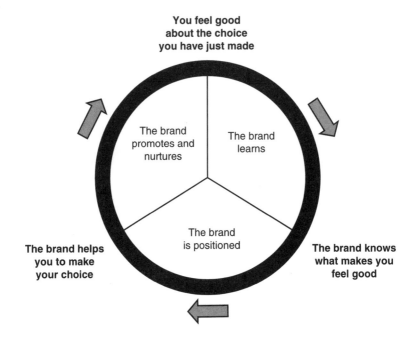

Figure PI.1 *The virtuous circle of a good brand*

Where brands came from... and why that matters

Go back 200 or 300 years and branding was something you did to a cow. A brand declared rights of property and ownership, and meant, particularly in a remote Scottish glen, '*keep your hands off*'. It is a nice irony that one of the identifying phenomena of the modern world should turn the word's meaning on its head – the 21st-century brand most determinedly declares '*get your hands on!*'.

From birth... to death?

What might the history of branding teach us? That today's brands are quite different in nature and intent from those which first emerged in the 19th century is clear, despite the continuity of so many names, from Cadbury to Kodak and Anchor to Omega. Brands, and the ideas behind brands, have evolved by learning to match the circumstances of the times. Managing this evolution is the essence of good brand management. Managing the changing purpose of brands is the essence of good marketing.

Promises, promises

Born in the 19th century as marks of authenticity in a new world of mass production, brands bowled into the 20th century like brash teenagers, full of bravado and promises. As consumers grew more 'brand literate', so the promises had to moderate and by mid-century brands had 'settled down' into steadier 'personalities'. Brand managers began to latch on to rather more single-minded claims as a means of giving direction to their brands.

The USP (unique selling proposition) was born, intended to give brands a very single-minded competitive advantage. Some USPs remain intact to this day – Volvo still 'owns' safety as a proposition in the car market, so much so that it has to try that much harder whenever it wants any message other than safety to be heard.

The brand image – the search for security

By the late 1950s, admen like David Ogilvy were looking to go beyond simple promises; they wanted to build 'brand image'. If a brand could build a better image than its competitors', then it would enjoy a degree of protection. A better product with an inferior image would struggle, and if its image could not be improved, it would fail. For some, the brand image was already more important than the product, a dangerous road to travel, leading to suspicions that branding is about masking inferior products with surface images.

Undoubtedly some brands still fall into this trap, but they are usually short-lived. Leaping ahead 50 years, the time taken to 'out' a hollow brand has reduced dramatically – just witness the litter of fallen dot.com brands.

The 'T Plan'

In the 1960s, the J Walter Thompson agency was working with its 'T Plan', an intellectual concept that regarded a brand as a synthesis of *knowledge, beliefs and emotional projections*. A brand was something that you knew about, that you might be able to state facts about – and facts that you believed to be true – and that engendered feelings and emotions that went well beyond the product or even its USP. Of the three ingredients, the emotional projections were most important.

Volvo might 'own' safety as its USP, but the emotional projections were even more important. This was safety with a purpose – the car would protect your family. In the end, it is this emotional projection, or what we might call the *'emotional charge'* of the brand, that gives Volvo its brand image and its brand value, not a list of cold statistics about crash tests or safety records.

Brands that elicit emotional responses were able to command premiums for longer. The brand was a route not only to competitive advantage but also to long-term security.

And into our own era...

At any one time in the closing decades of the last century, pundits were predicting either the imminent death of brands, or their rebirth through new business models.

On the side of death

First there was the rise and rise of private labels, the so-called 'no brands' that seemed to indicate a new medical condition among consumers – *'brand blindness'*. In 1991, advertising spending actually fell in the United States (a cataclysmic event in an industry that had grown from $50 billion to $130 billion in the previous decade), and then came 'Marlboro Friday'.

On 2 April 1993, Philip Morris slashed the price of Marlboro cigarettes in a price war with the 'no brands', and brands were declared dead by Wall Street. The share prices of big brand names across the board crashed as investors lost faith in what now looked like a dying phenomenon of the 20th century.

The 21st century seemed to promise a collage of big-value 'no brands', sold in personality-free discount warehouses, and an era of aggressive ad-bashing by street protesters, and more peacefully through the power of the TV remote control.

On the side of life – new business and brand models

The old model saw a brand essentially as a product with a wraparound of emotions and personality. The essential idea, or the soul of the brand, was slapped on the top. Figure 1.1 illustrates the typical 'product and surround' model, with the core being the product expressed at its most basic. Coca-Cola is simply a 'black sugared drink' at its core; its public face is built up like the layers of an onion.

The new model believes that brands can encompass entire lifestyles. The likes of Disney, Nike, The Body Shop, Starbucks

Figure 1.1 *The product and the surround*

and IKEA create emotional charges and experiences that go well beyond their products (and incidentally, the spend on advertising by such companies rose in the otherwise bleak advertising days of 1991). Note the retailers in the list; the sellers of 'no brands' were becoming brands in their own right.

Howard Shultz, CEO of Starbucks, sums it up: *'The people who line up for Starbucks aren't just there for the coffee.'* It might seem that the old model can still be applied to Starbucks – the core is a cup of coffee, the surround is the environment, the other customers, the location, etc. But the new breed of brand managers have tended to use their thought process in the other direction – finding products to fit a brand concept, rather than building layers on top of a product.

Does it make a difference which way round you think? For sure, and some brands have gone on to break 'the product and the surround' mould altogether, deciding that the manufacture of the product itself becomes less and less relevant. Tommy Hilfiger makes no products. It is run entirely on licensing agreements with products made by a range of commissioned suppliers, very often in South-East Asia.

Such new business and brand models raise many questions. Must a brand that tries to embrace a complete lifestyle be rooted in a business model that can itself sit happily within that lifestyle? Can a brand that might ooze with notions of liberation and well-being be based on exploitation at its source? More than this, can brands be created that exist free of any reference to the corporate body that creates and manages them? The argument is not so dissimilar (though less extreme perhaps) to the old one about painters and composers – could you love a painting or a concerto produced by a murderer? It depends on whether we know, and there are many out there determined that we should.

Nike

In a recent consumer promotion, Nike offered to place a chosen word or phrase next to the 'swoosh' logo on the customer's very own personalised pair of shoes. The promotion led to a heated boardroom discussion when one customer asked for their word: 'sweatshop'.

2

The brand as an emotional charge

Take a moment to flick through any magazine and try to find an example of an advert that pleases you, then perhaps one that annoys you, another that surprises you, one that might intrigue you, and you might even find one that persuades you. If you compared notes with someone else there's a good chance you will start a lively debate along the lines of 'how can you possibly think that… ', a debate which will highlight much about segmentation and targeting.

If any of the brands you looked at were 'big names', or at least well known to you, then you could probably express quite a lot of things about them – pieces of knowledge, ideas, thoughts, beliefs, promises, expectations and emotions, just from a few seconds glancing at a logo or a brand name. Chances are that the majority of what you could relate would be subjective rather than objective; you will more likely be able to discuss the *emotional charge* of the brand, and how it impacts on you, than its specific attributes. Try it with *your* favourite brand. Write down six or so things – how many facts, how many emotions?

What such an exercise makes clear is that the brand image is of course more than a picture or a logo; it is the range of associations triggered in your mind by that picture or logo, and those associations might be called the brand's *emotional charge*.

One of the strengths of a good brand is that it does all its best work inside your head. The emotional charge is a complex of the message sent and the impact of that message on the beliefs and needs of the customer. It manifests itself through the range and nature of the interactions the customer has with the brand.

Types of emotional charge: a model for discussing brands

We might define four types of emotional charge, each of them fairly broad, and then describe the main issues raised for the customer by that type of charge, and finally look at the role of the brand against each. Table 2.1 summarises this analysis.

Of course, there are crossovers between the levels, and brands that work on more than just one level – that is often their strength. Kellogg's is a guarantee of authenticity, but at the same time, while many consumers would fail to tell its corn-flakes from any other in a blind test, they will gain genuine *satisfaction* from pouring their favourite breakfast cereal from a reassuringly genuine Kellogg's box.

We will consider each of these levels of emotional charge, starting at the lowest and rising in intensity, illustrated by examples from FMCG (fast-moving consumer goods), B2B and service environments.

Table 2.1 Brands and the rising emotional charge

The *emotional charge*	The main issues for the customer	The role of the brand
A social expression	Will someone love me for loving it?	To facilitate conspicuity
Satisfaction or pleasure in use	Will I love it?	To win a premium price
A promise of performance in use	Will it do what I want it to do?	To influence choice
A guarantee of authenticity	Is it the real thing?	To make choice easy (even unthinking)

The brand as a guarantee of authenticity

Brands may have started life back in the 19th century as marks of authenticity but the notion is far from a dead one. It only takes an unstable market for the earliest forces behind branding to resurface.

Borjomi

In the days of the USSR, Borjomi sparkling mineral water was said to be the third-best-known brand in the Union; the Volga car and Aeroflot took the top spots. By 1996, after a decade or more of the kind of free enterprise that saw the rise of piracy and gangsterism, as much as 90 per cent of what went under the Borjomi label was said to be counterfeit. Then came the advertising campaign, reminding consumers of the distinctive packaging of the real Borjomi ('beware imitations'), and the not insignificant financial crisis of 1998 that killed off many of the poorly financed counterfeiters. By 2000, the claim was that 90 per cent of Borjomi sold was genuine. The company's revitalised fortunes show that branding as a mark of authenticity can still work wonders.

Examples

▨ **FMCG** – Kellogg's and the famous *'if it doesn't say Kellogg's on the pack, it isn't Kellogg's inside the pack'.*

▨ **B2B** – Hewlett-Packard replacement ink cartridges – *this will work, and it won't wreck those expensive printers you've just had installed.*

▨ **Service** – Citizens Advice Bureau – *the advice will be genuine.*

Of course, if authenticity was all it was about, who would ever *knowingly* buy an imitation Rolex watch? That people do (though few would admit to it) only shows that some brands work on much higher levels of emotional charge and that some people are prepared to lie, even to themselves, to reach those levels.

The brand as a promise of performance in use

If a brand makes a promise of performance then it must be able to prove it. Often the proof is in the longevity of the brand, but this can be a problem, as Coca-Cola found when it tried to launch a new formulation. New Coke was a flop for a host of reasons but one was undoubtedly the fact that many consumers felt a promise had been broken.

The higher the price tag or the higher the risk involved in the purchase, the more important is the promise. Some products give long lists of their features as proof, but good brands can achieve the same end more effectively. Who is persuaded by, or still more understands, the figures and the jargon that are so much a feature of advertisements for computer hardware? A simple statement that the computer has an 'Intel inside'® gives far greater assurance to most of us.

Durex

Condoms may print statistical evidence of their testing procedures on the packet, but for most people it is a matter of trusting in a particular brand name. When Durex started to market its more exotic range (the pursuit of satisfaction in use, not just performance), some consumers questioned for a moment whether the brand still retained its absolute trustworthiness and reliability. It is not always easy for a brand to change an emotional charge that has become firmly attached.

Examples

▓ **FMCG** – Fairy Liquid's famous comparison tests, or the Duracell battery in the Christmas toy that goes on, and on, and on...
▓ **B2B** – A brand such as Lycra promises performance on two levels: as a high performance raw material for a clothing manufacturer, and as an aid to sales of that clothing through its strong consumer franchise.

■ **Service** – Accenture or Pricewaterhouse-Coopers have brands that are able to promise performance through the 'honour role' of their client list.

The brand as satisfaction: pleasure or fulfilment in use

One of the best examples of a brand acting as an aid to satisfaction is the label on a bottle of wine. Simply seeing the bottle, if we recognise the name and think well of it, can convince us that the taste will be, and is, good. Try it for yourself in an open and then a blind test and just see if it isn't true.

There is plenty of hard evidence that headache sufferers will feel better treated by taking a brand of analgesic that they have heard of rather than an unknown generic. Placebos masquerading as well-known brands have been shown to be more effective than placebos in plain white boxes.

Persil

Can a washing powder be elevated to the level of satisfaction or fulfilment? The folk at Persil believe so and have for many years positioned their brand as something more than the route to clean clothes. The inference of the Persil message is that it is the route to a clean family, so putting the user into the role of protector and carer. If this doesn't quite put washing on a par with eating chocolate or watching movies, by injecting that element of pride into using the brand it certainly raises it above that of plain drudgery. Many people will pay a good premium for such an elevating thought...

Examples

▤ **FMCG** – Dulux paint, not just colour for your walls but a means of *'transforming your home'*, or Titleist golf balls – just having them in your bag makes you feel better about your golf.

▤ **B2B** – *'Nobody ever got fired for buying IBM'*. This famous phrase makes plain that commercial buyers buy on more than product performance – there is also the question of job security. At the same time, there is the potential thought that nobody set the world alight by buying IBM. This illustrates one of the problems of a stable image, of an unchanging emotional charge – it puts you up there to be shot at, to be shown as the old fuddy-duddy by the new kids on the block.

▤ **Service** – INSIGHT Marketing and People. It is not unusual in the training business to have someone ring you and say that they want their team to go through one of your courses because 10 years ago *they* went on it and they still remember the good time they had, and the amount they learnt, and the great trainers, and the use it has been since...

The brand as a social expression: ego, conformity/nonconformity

Certain brands have always been good for those in pursuit of recognition through their purchasing behaviour. Driving a new Jaguar, wearing an old Barbour jacket, carrying those green plastic bags from Harrods (even when shopping in Asda), these are all very characteristic statements of the conspicuous consumer.

Of course, Jaguars are good cars, Barbours good coats and Harrods a fine shop, so how much is conspicuity the motivation? Take away the symbols and the brand names, put a Ford badge on the very same car, an Asda Mr George label inside the same coat, and Somerfield on the same bags, and just see how many buyers would shift their allegiances very quickly.

Brands that make social expressions relate to the customer's confidence about themselves, but in a complex way. For some, the designer label is a confident statement about who they are, while for others it is a desire to belong to a recognised group that is born out of insecurity. Sometimes we like to have our purchasing decisions 'approved', and while seeing others wearing the same designer jeans might upset some, for others it says – *'whew, I did the right thing'*.

The subtext of many car advertisements is more about reassuring you that you have in fact already made the right decision and it will be respected by your peers, than it is about trying to influence you to buy in the first place.

Social expression can be about conformity or nonconformity, and brands can fit either of these positions. Drinking Pimm's on ice in an East End pub can set you apart from the crowd, while Hofmeister lager will make you one of the lads (for the reverse scenario imagine carrying a can of Hofmeister around Henley Regatta...).

Hofmeister

Hofmeister was launched successfully in the United Kingdom, targeted at young working-class males in London, pretty much a closed shop where beer is concerned and group conformity is the key to buying behaviour. Hofmeister used George the bear, a 'dude', to gain it street credibility, and of course those who don't see the appeal of George just aren't in the target segment.

Examples

▓ **FMCG** – Rolex, Rémy Martin, and the explosion of 'logo brands', especially on clothing – there is now even a 'no logo' brand...

▓ **B2B** – Gore-Tex allows the clothing manufacturer to make its claim of superiority while enabling the consumer to be identified with 'those in the know'.

■ **Service** – Diners Club is said to say something about the user, and saying that is saying it all.

Finding your level

It might seem from looking at these examples that a brand would always want to appeal at the highest level of emotional charge, but this is not always the wisest ambition. For one thing, sustaining a brand image at the level of a social expression is an expensive activity and requires a continuity of credibility over a long period. Entry costs are always high, but they rise dramatically as the intensity of the emotional charge increases. And then, the higher the emotional charge, the more precise your positioning, so the more you leave yourself open to changing times.

Rather than simply aspiring to the highest level, it is more sensible to recognise what level is realistic for your brand and your resources, and then to excel at that level. Determining what is realistic is not easy; the factors that contribute to the level of emotional charge that a brand might reach are many and complex. There are no real rules, and even if there were, we would only find the world awash with examples of brands that break them. Perhaps we might attempt to boil it down to two admittedly rather broad, but hugely important, factors. The emotional charge likely to be achieved by a brand is the result of: 1) what that brand does to build its image – **brand activity** – and 2) how customers relate to the brand – **customer interaction.**

The strongest brands are those that most successfully pull these two strands together, managing the customer's interactions through the brand's activity, and all in the direction of the intended image and emotional charge.

Brand activity

Some brands clearly do more about building their image than others. This isn't just a question of money, it is about consistency and good use of the past.

Fairy Liquid

Fairy Liquid held a children's competition to celebrate the millennium asking kids to redesign its famous 'Bizzy' logo, the baby with the towelling nappy. Unsurprisingly, the winning images were very space age and appeared on 'limited edition' bottles. As a means of reinforcing a part of the brand heritage and its emotional charge, at minimal cost, while creating new interest, this was a branding tour de force.

And then, they changed the bottle. No more summer Saturday squeezy bottle fights on the back lawn, and no more Blue Peter-inspired pencil holders for father's day. Is this throwing away the heritage, or is it building a new one that is more in tune with the times? The new bottles are distinctive in a supermarket environment where retailers have done their best to ape the brand leaders. It feels like a quality product, with a cleverly designed grip around the waist – for hands that do dishes and with a nod towards Jean-Paul Gaultier's famous perfume – and Bizzy is still there...

Of course brands must change, as must products. Nobody would expect a Sony product to be the same today as it was just two years ago. Is that product renewal or brand renewal? The answer is that it is both – some brands are about being up to date. Equally, we would all like to think that Cadbury's chocolate was the same as it was when we were kids, and indeed for some of their range the product changes themselves may be relatively minor – some brands are about being as good as they ever were. But don't be misled, the Cadbury's brand managers have not been sleeping for 30 years...

Sponsorship and PR are part of the plan for raising the 'emotional charge' of a brand. The link between cigarette brands and sporting events (a historical oddity of the 1970s and 1980s) was always a great deal more than an awareness campaign. While few were moved to believe that cigarettes were actually good for you as a result of the emotional projections, many were 'relaxed' in their habit by these good associations.

Personalities attached to the brand can do all sorts of things for the emotional charge, whether it's Tina Turner or Jack Dee. And if the personality can be home-grown, all the better – Victor Kiam did wonders for Remington shavers (so good he bought the company), and Virgin was made all the more powerful as a brand just because Sir Richard Branson kept trying to take a balloon around the world, and had longish hair...

Of course, some brands manage to get along with doing very little – no linked promotions, no advertising, just the continuation of a heritage built up by a previous generation of brand managers. This can be a very low-cost approach to brand management, and why spend money if it isn't needed? The truth of the matter with such brands, however, is that they are only as good as their lack of competition allows them to be. Enter a competitor, and make it one with a good deal of energy, and old-established brands can disappear fast. Many an FMCG grocery brand back in the 1970s and 1980s gave ample space for the growth of the supermarket's own label.

Customer interaction

Brands can pour millions into urging their customers to interact with them, and get very little return. It seems that some brands are just better suited to higher levels of interaction and higher levels of emotional response than others. The answer doesn't lie in the promotional budget (at least, not to start with) but in the customer's circumstances as a buyer, and how that conditions their perceptions.

You might love Gucci if you have plenty of money and need to show people how successful you are, be indifferent to it if you have just enough money to buy that sensible pair of shoes you have had your eyes on for some time, or hate it if you have little money and despise conspicuous consumption.

Of course, you may have little money and dream of the day you could afford Gucci. The interaction between income level and brand attitudes is not a simple equation, and therein lies an important feature of branding – aspiration.

The purchasing behaviour of consumers cannot be reduced to an assessment of their wealth. In any case, wealth is relative. More Jaguar S-Types are sold to people who can't really afford the car, but are determined to arrange their finances to make sure that they can, just, than to those with more than adequate funds.

The aspiration factor is of huge significance in branding. Walk around any run-down district of a big city and see what the kids are wearing. Logos abound. The 'living large' philosophy of the hip-hop generation, particularly in the United States and often in poor inner-city communities, is expressed by wearing the likes of Tommy Hilfiger clothes or Timberland shoes, clothes that win their wearers status through an association with lifestyles well out of their financial league.

A host of factors might determine the nature of these interactions and so the potential level of emotional charge. Figure 2.1 lists just some of them.

- the price paid;
- the budget available;
- the percentage of your budget involved;
- the frequency of purchase;
- the risks involved in use;
- the consipicuity of the purchase;
- the consumer's desire to make a statement;
- the consumer's aspirations;
- the importance of consistency;
- the utility of the product or service;
- the tangibility of performance;
- the number of brands competing for attention;
- the number of interactions with the brand.

Figure 2.1 *Factors that determine the level and nature of customer interactions*

Multiple interactions

The last factor listed in Figure 2.1, the number of interactions with the brand, is a factor that has come increasingly to the fore with the rise of so-called superbrands. These are often found in the world of fashion and clothing (Nike, Tommy Hilfiger), and in retailing and entertainment (Gap, Starbucks, Disney, Sky). These brands have something of an advantage over the likes of Persil or MacLean's when it comes to building the emotional charge. The range and complexity of interactions gives these brands a much greater opportunity to grab our attention and our emotions. Disneyworld has got you from check-in to check-out, Starbucks might keep you for a full hour, some clothes we might wear all week – but we brush our teeth for only a few minutes a day…

The role of the brand manager is to be ever vigilant for opportunities to increase the level and complexity of the customer's interactions. The Persil 'care line' is an attempt to interact with its customers on a level beyond tipping powder into a machine. Advising people on how to store a treasured wedding dress (wrap it in brown paper…) has an emotional value well beyond soap powder. We might only spend a few minutes each day brushing our teeth, but we can be made to think about them, and what assaults them, all day.

The factors listed in Figure 2.1 don't work in isolation and nor do they always work in the same direction. Just because an item is low priced, regularly purchased, and has a utilitarian purpose, that doesn't mean that a brand can't have a high-level emotional charge. Toilet paper is a case in point.

Andrex

The Andrex brand builds emotional responses that go well beyond the everyday utilitarian factors. The Andrex puppies exude messages of softness, warmth, care and responsibility, while at the same time helping to communicate messages about the length of the roll. It is a subtle blend with a strong appeal. It is also a very neat solution to the problem of 'taste' in saying what you need to say about such a product.

The virtuous circle

Brand activity builds the nature of the customer interaction. The two factors become intertwined, the virtuous circle shown at the start of Part I and repeated as Figure 2.2. The outcome is a powerful brand.

The key phrase in this model is 'The brand learns'. Brand activity is not enough, customer interaction is not enough. The quest for the holy grail of branding is about understanding how these two things interact, and learning as you proceed.

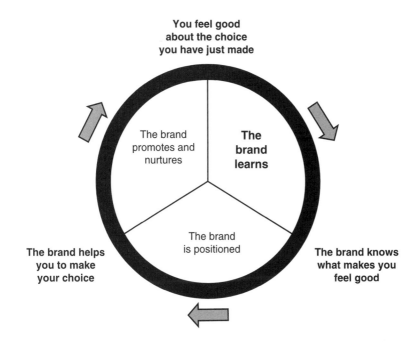

Figure 2.2   *The virtuous circle of a good brand*

Kleenex

Shortly after the First World War, Kimberley Clark launched a brand in the United States called Kleenex. The company had a surplus of cellucotton (used as the filter in gas masks) and believed it had found an outlet. The war was over, people were after a little gaiety, and sales of make-up boomed. Kleenex was launched as the ideal make-up remover, and very good it was, but the brand hardly set the world alight. There was a good deal of brand activity but to no avail, this was a small market and there were plenty of alternatives.

Then the folk at Kleenex started to listen to their customers, and they discovered a whole new set of interactions going on that were not only unexpected, but in truth filled some of them with dismay. People were using Kleenex to blow their noses. Fine, there's a market out there, but how do you promote such a product? The answer was to let the brand evolve.

Existing customers had certain 'polite' expectations of Kleenex and nose-blowing messages might cause some disturbance, so the first step was to target a different audience, and who better than children – they of the runny noses.

Parents were encouraged to buy Kleenex for their kids to stop them being antisocial and unhygienic – a tall order, but Kleenex it seemed had the answer. In the 1930s Kleenex hit on the slogan *'Don't put a cold in your pocket'* and the adult market was hooked. The brand's positioning was changed from a niche market to a mass market, and it did it through a process of learning and evolving – a vital quality of any successful brand.

Brand evolution and brand definition

There is another kind of virtuous circle that we might find helpful in understanding how brands acquire their emotional charge. Indeed, we can go beyond the idea of an emotional charge to identify what we might call the brand definition.

Brand definition is the sum of a number of different overlapping aspects of the brand, referred to by a variety of terms. People talk of the idea behind the brand, we have spoken of its emotional charge, others talk of its essence, its soul, or even what we will call in Chapter 15, the brand's DNA.

Brands evolve in response to changing customer expectations (if they are listening brands), and those expectations are in turn prompted and managed by the very process of evolution. Out of this process comes the brand definition. This is illustrated in Figure 2.3.

If brands are a result of their history, then what is the role of the brand manager? Is evolution to be prodded, accelerated, retarded, or just accepted?

Levi Strauss

In the 1970s, Levi Strauss attempted to move into the formal menswear market with the Levi name sown into off-the-peg suits – Levi Tailored Classics. The market research warned the company against it: 'People are not ready for such a big step – why not try separates first?', but it went ahead and paid the price of forcing a brand into territory that was not yet ready. People had expectations of the brand, and this move didn't fit.

Figure 2.3 *Brand definition and brand evolution*

Of course, from time to time 'acting' works. People had no expectations of 3M's Post-it notes before they were launched, so it had to be 'action'. It worked, but we haven't space for the list of the failures from such an approach. From time to time, we will hail a revolutionary new concept or a breakthrough brand – Amazon.com perhaps – as the result of action rather than reaction.

With a circular process, the brand managers can jump in wherever they choose, acting or reacting. Brands said to be 'before their time' are generally brands that acted rather than reacted, forcing the brand definition on to the market, rather than allowing it to evolve with that market. Reacting reduces the risk of failure, but also increases the risk of being overtaken by competitors – a delicate balance.

3

The brand as a personality

A useful exercise is to ask people to create a collage of the pictures and words that represent their idea of the brand in question. The purpose is to have people express their perceptions of that brand without having to use a vocabulary borrowed from the psychoanalyst or anthropologist. Brands can of course be described in such terms, and probably will be by the advertising agency, but most customers would be unlikely, unable or unwilling to do so, and it is the customers' perceptions we want to understand.

Identify a group of six or eight people from your target market – customers and potential customers – and sit them down in front of a pile of newspapers and magazines – everything from *Horse and Hound* to *Hello!*. Arm them with scissors and glue, and ask each of them to cover an A1-sized sheet of paper with the words and images they feel are most appropriate to your brand.

You are not concerned here with their artistic skill, but with the associations your brand conjures in their mind. Are they good or bad associations, and more to the point, are they the associations that you intend? Their creations will often surprise you, sometimes disappoint you, and just sometimes they might depress you.

Let's say your product is an upmarket non-alcoholic cocktail drink. It can be an unsettling exercise when the brand you aim to position as an aspirational 'taste experience' with connotations of good health is illustrated with pictures of mushy peas or pot-bellied 'lads' out on the town. Unsettling, but this is something you need to know – is the brand coming across to the customer as you intend?

People may choose to use other brands' images in their collage, suggesting parallels in values and beliefs that may be useful to the brand manager. If the other brands used are close competitors, then perhaps your own positioning is not yet sufficiently precise? If the brands used are far removed from your own, then this may simply be an opportunity for some creative stealing – professionals call it research.

Most commonly, pictures of people are used, making strong links between the looks and the character of a brand and the looks and character of a person. Describing the brand as a personality is of huge importance: people can identify with people – they can love them, but they can also hate them…

In developing the essence of your brand, its appeal and its presence, personality is a valuable touchstone. You will have a particular personality in mind, perhaps a real person, and this collage exercise will help to show how close you are getting.

Who is your brand?

This brings us to another exercise. Ask a group of people, ideally a focus group of customers and potential customers, to say 'who' your brand would be if it was, say:

■ a movie star;
■ a comedian;
■ a newsreader;
■ a politician;
■ a sportsperson;
■ a writer;
■ a TV 'personality';
■ a game show host.

You might even ask:

▓ Is it male or female?
▓ How old are they?
▓ What are their politics?
▓ What religion do they follow?
▓ Are they married with kids, or single?
▓ How's their health?
▓ How do they respond to stress and crisis?

Deciphering the answers to these questions and interpreting the collage exercise is not an easy task, and will be best done by professionals. Amateur observers, particularly those closely involved, have a knack of seeing whatever they happen to be looking for.

With the help of a professional market researcher (experienced in brand positioning) to pose the questions and assess the results, exercises like these will help you to construct a personality profile of your brand. Importantly, this will be a genuine personality as perceived by your customers, not a wish list as defined in your marketing plan. Then come the hard questions:

▓ Is this what you aimed for?
▓ If not, is it close enough?
▓ If not, how can we close the gap?
▓ If not, might the described personality actually be preferable? It is, after all, already established in the customer's mind...

Why seeing the brand as a personality helps

Seeing the brand as a personality has many advantages for the brand manager. Brands seek particular responses from the customer, and people respond to people almost better than any other stimulant. Figure 3.1 is a model that sees brands as representing different levels of personal relationships.

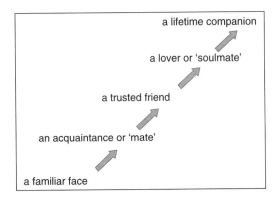

Figure 3.1   *The brand as a personal relationship*

And the point of such a model? Well, we can see that people will expect more from a lover or a life companion than someone they consider just a familiar face. We can also see that the loyalty they will give in return will differ hugely. A brand that is considered to be a good mate, but no more, can make some realistic estimates of its value and its resilience to competition, and it can make plans on how to become a trusted friend.

4

The brand as a mark of loyalty

Brands can build astonishing loyalty, the value of which should not be lightly dismissed. Many businesses without strong brands would love to escape from the methods that they have to adopt in search of such loyalty.

True loyalty does not result from monopoly. Watch how customers will jump ship, almost regardless of the relative merits of the new offer, when a new player enters the field previously held by a monopoly. British Gas lost many of its industrial customers when deregulation came in, and much the same happened to British Telecom up against a sudden wave of new providers. In time, many of them come back, but only as a result of some expensive coaxing, not because of loyalty.

True loyalty does not result from bribery. Retailer loyalty cards, credit card membership reward schemes, air miles – these are all bribery, and when the bribe is withdrawn or the novelty wears off, the customer looks elsewhere.

True loyalty does not result from discounting. Many studies have shown that when consumers buy a discounted product for reasons of price alone, they still yearn to buy the higher-priced, big brand name alternative, but money won out this time – just wait until they win the lottery…

When looking at the costs of branding, you should consider the costs of winning loyalty through these kinds of alternatives. What will it cost to keep competitors out through the maintenance of an effective monopoly, to lock customers in through rebates or rewards, or to keep them through continual price discounting?

True loyalty – what is it, and how far can it go?

True loyalty results from the quality of the relationship built between the supplier and the customer. If this involves direct human contact then there are significant opportunities to build loyalty through personal behaviour, but in the absence of that, the brand is the main and most effective representation of the relationship.

Customer expectations and loyalty

We will consider two variables that help to determine the customer's expectations and so help define the level and type of loyalty they may show for a brand. These are the significance of the purchase to the customer, and the amount of money involved.

Significance and brand awareness

The significance of the brand to the customer results from a number of factors, but perhaps principally the following two: 1) the more complex the relationship the customer has with the brand, represented by the number and variety of the brand interactions, the greater the chance of building long-lasting loyalty; 2) the more the brand can identify with the customer's pressing issues – getting under their skin – the more chance for building long-lasting loyalty. And the significance of 'significance' to awareness and loyalty? Let's just compare some items of equal expense, but with rather different levels of significance.

A refrigerator versus a cooker. The fridge is just for storing things, while the cooker is for creating things – brand awareness and the significance of branding for cookers is far greater than it is for refrigerators.

A bed versus a hi-fi. A bed is for sleeping, and is covered up for most of its life. The hi-fi is for entertaining, even for performing, and is on show to all those to be entertained. Bed manufacturers go to great efforts to brand their products, but I challenge you to name three bed brands in the space of time you can name six brands of hi-fi.

The brand manager wishing to increase brand loyalty will do well to examine the relative significance of the brand, and the number and nature of the customer interactions. If they can increase those interactions then they have a good chance of increasing the brand's significance and so the customer's loyalty.

The brands that inspire the most loyalty are those that are most significant to the customer as a result of their high level of involvement and the impact on their 'hot spots'. Motor cars have a lot going for them in this regard, involving the customer through a long cycle of interactions, from anticipation, to selection, to purchase, to use, and even on to memory of that use. Reduce the number of interactions, reduce the significance to the customer, and loyalty gets harder to win. Some purchases just make it plain difficult to be loyal.

Relative spend

Having considered the significance of the purchase, let us now link that to a second variable – the amount of money spent on the purchase relative to all other expenditure. These two variables form the two axes of a matrix shown in Figure 4.1. I have then suggested some items that I would put in each box of the matrix, based on my own perceptions and expenditure.

You may disagree with my positioning; perhaps for you baked beans are a vital purchase and getting the wrong brand is a minor disaster – perhaps you have children... and this is the whole point about understanding consumer expectations,

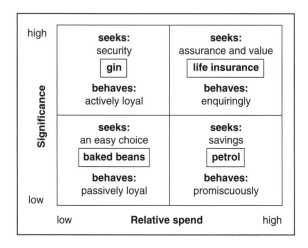

Figure 4.1 *Loyalty, based on the brand's significance and size of expenditure*

branding and loyalty. Different groups of consumers have different expectations, and if we wish a brand to be relevant then we have to be targeting the right groups; branding and segmentation, as we shall observe time and again, are quite inseparable. Rather than using my examples, position some of your own purchases on the matrix and then ask yourself some questions:

▨ Do you go about purchasing these items in the same way, or differently?
▨ What do you expect from a product or service positioned in each box?
▨ What 'value' are you seeking?
▨ How loyal would you be to a brand in each box?

The answers will demonstrate how brand values must be positioned dependent on the consumer's expectations, and that those expectations depend on how the consumer positions you in their 'mental map', as represented by the matrix.

Table 4.1 takes the items from the matrix and, based on the value sought by the consumer and their likely level of loyalty,

Table 4.1 Expectations, loyalty and branding

Item	The consumer seeks	Likely kind of loyalty	Possible branding approach
gin	security	actively loyal	retain loyalty – 'confidence' *'It's got to be Gordon's'*
baked beans	an easy choice	passively loyal	make loyalty easy *'Beanz Meanz Heinz'*
life insurance	assurance and value	enquiringly	earn loyalty – 'trust' *'Because life is complicated enough'*
petrol	savings	promiscuously	'lock in' *Texaco Reward Card*: *'It's a bribe, but it's a good bribe.'*

adds a comment on the possible branding approach. The good brand acts appropriately for the value sought and the likely level of loyalty. It doesn't try to force unreasonable loyalty, it acts according to the type of loyalty it can expect, including bribery where necessary.

Brands can of course act to increase their significance by various means, some more long-lasting than others. For me, Esso and Shell have little to distinguish between them, and attempts to differentiate their products through technical claims leave me cold. But if one brand adds a shop to its station, with a cash machine, and clean toilets, then perhaps it will win my loyalty, until the other brand matches it...

Adding to the product element of the brand is often less effective than other actions, and it is also relatively easy to copy. The addition of services can have a greater impact, and, for me at least, a longer-lasting loyalty might be built if I were to identify one brand as more environmentally sensitive, or as a more responsible employer – the link between the brand image and the reality of the company behind the brand. But then that's just me.

5

The brand as evidence of your unique competitive advantage

The brand helps a business to represent, in a single focused definition, what is perhaps the most important purpose of marketing – the pursuit of a unique competitive advantage. A pictorial definition of the purpose and practice of marketing is shown in Figure 5.1.

Marketing is a matching process between the capabilities of the supplier and the needs of the market or customer, in pursuit of a profitable competitive advantage. The company's capabilities are as they exist today, or how they could be developed. The needs of the market may be real or they may be latent – perhaps requiring a little push to bring them to the surface.

The marketer's task is to find the match between these two pursuits and, most importantly, to do it better than the competition, who are chasing down just the same road. The more unique the match can be, provided it is a genuine match of real capabilities and real needs, the better the chance for competitive advantage. It is of little advantage, or profit, to find a match

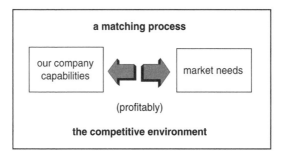

Figure 5.1 *Marketing – its purpose and practice*

that your competitors can copy, and perhaps ultimately achieve at lower costs than you.

The brand manager's task is to help develop this match and represent its uniqueness through the uniqueness of the brand. Brands will live and prosper so long as they continue to express a unique match between real needs and real capabilities. As needs change, as they almost always do, so must the supplier's capabilities, and so must the brand. The brand must evolve if it is to continue evidencing this unique match. Brands wither and die when either they fail to evolve, or when the capabilities behind them fail to keep pace with the changing needs of the market.

Dyson

Hoover owned the vacuum cleaner market in the United Kingdom for most of the last century; it even 'owned the word' for vacuuming. It lost this unquestioned ownership to Dyson because its brand definition rested on its laurels. It failed to spot a potential update in the matching process even when it was placed under its nose. Dyson had observed a latent customer desire for better suction and less messy disposal, and offered Hoover his 'cyclone system' invention. It was turned down because its bagless solution threatened Hoover's lucrative market for replacement bags. Now it is the Dyson brand that owns the best and most unique match between capabilities and need.

Brands need to be more than 'surface fluff'

'*Brands define who you are.*' If this is true, then either brands have become a dangerously overblown device for social control, or customers have succumbed to some wretched wasting disease that affects their sense of identity. Fortunately, it isn't.

Sure, people buy brands that they like, brands that make them feel good, and brands that tune into what they want out of life – but they don't become the sum of their purchases. If they do, then they should seek counselling. People's needs and aspirations define what brands are, not the other way round, and any brand manager beguiled by the '*brands maketh man*' mantra, or the cry of '*we're all just dream merchants*', will more than likely get their brands into an arrogant and pretentious mess.

Aspirations are important in branding, and nobody wants to see dowdy presentation or uninspiring advertising copy, but the dream merchant approach too often tries to manufacture something out of nothing. '*All mouth and no trousers*' is not a bad comment on a brand that attempts to exist only on its image. The success of a brand lies in the way that it builds a powerful image around a genuine and convincing offer. In the long run, no offer means no brand.

6

The rise and rise of the retail brand

The fact that retailers sell other people's brands has tended to obscure the fact that they are themselves some of the most potent brands ever created.

The private label slur

The brand managers of the big FMCG 'product brands' used to be very superior in their attitude to retailers, for decades regarding them simply as their channel to market. When the retailers had the temerity to launch products under their own names, these efforts were dismissed as 'no brands'.

Certainly the early days of the own label were somewhat hit and miss. Quality was hugely variable, particularly as suppliers were changed at a rate that made any kind of consistency almost impossible. But soon, retailers were reducing the choice on the shelf to the brand leader and their own-label alternative. For suppliers, being the brand leader became all that mattered, and making own labels could only be a distraction, or a bolt hole for the now displaced number two and three brands. The result of such analysis could only be conflict between supplier and customer.

Proprietary brands versus the retailer's brand

Own label was becoming a potent force, and yet still it was belittled. When the number two brands were forced out of the game by the retailers' two brand policy, and the likes of Crosse & Blackwell withdrew entirely from tinned vegetables, it was reckoned to be a defeat at the hands of Heinz, the brand leader – but wasn't it really a defeat at the hands of the retailers' own growing brands?

With the retailers' own labels being the proprietary brands' biggest competition, a new dilemma arose – their biggest customers were also their biggest competitors. It was a dilemma that occupied a good portion of the brand manager's thinking time. To make these products would be a sign of defeat, they argued, and feeling better for that decision closed their eyes once again to what was going on before them.

Quality and consistency of own labels improved, the imitation of branded packaging design became rife and throughout the 1990s many branded suppliers were speaking with their lawyers almost as frequently as with their customers.

The proprietary brands labour under many disadvantages to the retailers' own labels. In most cases, they are no longer allowed to place their own point-of-sale materials in store. The result is that the own label, designed for the environment it will be sold in, often looks more at home than the brand leader.

The retailer will often place its own product in the prime location, with the brand leader on a lower or higher shelf, explaining to its brand leader suppliers that if there is such a clear consumer demand for their products then those consumers will surely make the effort to search them out.

While the stature of proprietary brands can be diminished by the retailers' activities, they can also lose out at the other end of the competitive struggle – the retail brand can be more cavalier with cost-cutting measures than they. If Andrex shrinks the size of its toilet roll to boost its margins then the whole country will notice, and protests will be heard in a thousand bus queues – it sometimes even makes prime-time television. If the retailer does the same with its own label, then that's only to be expected of an own label, isn't it? A proprietary brand still has to behave as if it's better quality than the own label, even if it isn't – and that costs.

Squeezed at both ends, branded suppliers in the 1990s were at last persuaded to dance to the retailer's tune. Category management became the great cry, and brands were told that they must work within the retailer's chosen environment, and to do so meant working alongside the own label, not against it. This allowed the own label to move away from its image as the cheaper, but lower-quality, alternative, and begin its development as an alternative choice on grounds of its own innovation and value.

Branded sausages

There was a famous study done in the 1980s that demonstrated how when the proportion of branded sausages in the freezer cabinet was reduced to a certain level, total sausage sales would start to fall. The brands, it was shown, provided the necessary innovation to keep the category healthy. Look today in the freezer cabinet and chances are that the exciting things happening with sausages are happening inside an own-label wrapper. (The Porkinson banger and the Wall's 'Instants' sausage are notable exceptions, but often hidden from view in deference to the retailer's own Lincolnshire herb, organic hand-reared low-fat chipolatas…)

At last the branded suppliers began to realise that what they were witnessing was the growth of a new kind of brand, not a *me too, lukewarm imitation, no brand*, but a complex and increasingly innovative multifaceted brand – a retail brand.

The multifaceted brand

Now it is clear that the products sold under the own label represent just a part of what has become a remarkably multifaceted brand. The retailer has some huge advantages when it comes to branding, compared to even the biggest FMCG suppliers with the biggest budgets. If the emotional charge and power of a brand is the result of its interactions with its customers, then we can see how Sainsbury's or Asda might be able to outbrand a packet of cornflakes; they have so much more to play with. Let's go shopping – there is the free car park, the architecture of the store, the music, the staff, the restaurant, the offers and the savings, and more than groceries, the car insurance, holidays and financial investments. Some retailers turn their stores into shows – the 'retail theatre' of The Disney Store, with its greeters and its sing-along video wall.

Of course, we might not even have ventured out of the house, but shopped from home by the internet, logging on to a retailer's site where the ability to build its own multifaceted but coherent brand offer at the expense of the necessarily fragmented proprietary brands is even greater.

Getting the upper hand...

Time was when retailers knew about handling stock and building displays, and brands knew about customers. The retailers eagerly accepted the market research carried out by the brands, and their offer was effectively decided for them. All that has changed, largely as a result of the EPOS data gathered by barcode scanners and embellished by the further information from loyalty cards. Retailers have a knowledge of consumers that is second to none, and they use it to position and target their spectacularly multifaceted brand offers.

The consumer's champion?

Tesco fought a high-profile campaign against a number of brands, most notably Levi Strauss, in aiming to offer branded goods at discount prices. It labelled its campaign 'rip-off Britain', arguing that the big brands were using restrictive practices to keep their products at premium prices. Levi responded by arguing that the environment in which you purchase the jeans – '*the last nine yards of cable*' was its phrase – is an important part of the product and its image and should not be left in the hands of the discounting supermarket. One has to suspect both sides' motives. We are looking neither at the consumer's champion nor at the upholder of sacred brand values; rather this is a fight for the dominance of product or retail brands. At present, some aspects of the law stand behind the product brand in this kind of dispute, but much of the press is increasingly aligned behind the retailer. Of course, this particular battle has only just begun.

The death of proprietary brands?

Does the rise and rise of the retail brand imply the decline and fall of the proprietary brand? Probably not, provided that the suppliers recognise the challenge and evolve their brands accordingly. It shouldn't be supposed that the retailers have it all their own way. Their customers have certain expectations of what they will find in store, particularly with regard to certain brand names – their favourites, the big names, the recently promoted – and if they are disappointed, then they may just change the store they shop in. In this regard, a supermarket with no Coca-Cola is rather like a pub with no beer.

Consumer brands still have a power over retailers, but only if they continue to behave as consumer brands – understanding the needs of their target customers, coming up with the goods, and investing in communicating that achievement.

There are signs that many are not sure of how to proceed along this path, as if stunned by the changes they have witnessed. When Tesco decided that it would sell its hugely valuable EPOS data to its suppliers, many of those suppliers were at a loss as to what to do with those data. Having once been the consumer expert, building successful brands based on a genuine match between their capabilities as manufacturers and the consumer's needs as uncovered by their research, it is as if a decade of category management has left them witless. Category management has sometimes been used as a weapon to weaken the franchise held by consumer brands, and too many branded suppliers have been seduced into believing that a successful brand is just the outcome of a big promotional budget. At least retailers know better.

7

The B2B and service brand – branding is not just for FMCG

Too many companies in B2B or service industries dismiss branding as a viable option. Here are just some of the stated reasons, with some counter-comments to each:

- *'Brands are just names, logos or slogans, and such things are irrelevant to our customer's choice of a supplier.'*
  A good brand is much more than a name, logo or slogan, but even so, don't underestimate the human element in your customers' decision-making process. They respond to good-quality promotion like anyone else, and don't be surprised if your anonymity and timidity leave them agog with indifference.
- *'Brands are for products, and while we do have different products it is really the company that they are buying.'*
  Chapter 13 will discuss the idea of the corporate brand, very often a good model for the B2B market where common values support each and all of its product offers.

▓ *'Brands are only needed when there is no tangible differ-ence. The point about our business is that we have a real point of difference...'*
Brands that depend solely on an image are vulnerable, and short-lived when something tangibly better comes along. If you really do have a point of competitive advantage then you have the basis for a strong brand. So you're great, but how many times can you tell the customer how great you are? Most probably, you haven't done so in years, just hoping that they remember. A brand can help you express that real point of difference every time the customer inter-acts with it.

▓ *'B2B decisions are tangible and based on logic; there is no room for emotion in our business, our customers work on facts and experience...'*
If this really is so, then make your brand definition tangible and logical but, as before, don't underestimate the human-ity of your customers... Trust is an emotion, confidence is an emotion, and both are usually key to a successful B2B or service brand. A good brand can express its trustworthi-ness through its consistency and level-headed approach. When promoting the B2B brand, don't make the mistake of trying to replicate the necessary and valuable emotional excitement of the FMCG world with unnecessary and devaluing hype.

▓ *'FMCG brands only have to convince an individual, we have to convince the whole company. Sometimes the deci-sion-making unit extends from the boardroom to the postroom. This calls for creative selling by a team of people with initiative, not branding.'*
Even more need, then, for a set of values that will determine your whole approach. Each contact must be tailored but ultimately there must be consistency in the message. If each individual in your team represents the essence of your proposition then this gives huge strength to the relationship. It also gives you a brand definition.

▓ *'Consumer brands are about quick sales based on impulse decisions. We might wait a year or more for a decision.'*
Consumers might dwell on their choice of hi-fi or motor car for years, and the suppliers of such goods recognise the huge value of a strong brand that can hold the potential customer's attention for these lengths of time.

▓ *'Listening to the "dream merchant" and the "brands define who you are" brigade makes me want to laugh, or be sick. They have obviously never met the buyers we have to deal with.'*
Try to put them out of your mind; they don't represent the vast majority of brand activities. Don't even think of working with a branding consultant, advertising agency or other professional that talks in these terms. Moreover, regard the presence of professional and testing buyers as something that will help keep your brand definition genuine and robust.

▓ *'Our customers make it very clear that price is all that matters.'*
Are you sure that you are not the victim of a professional buyer's little piece of theatre? Have you spoken to anyone other than the buyer, and if so, do they all think the same? Perhaps some care more about costs than price? If it *really* is just about price, how about developing a 'never knowingly undersold' brand definition?

▓ *'You need millions before a brand means anything – just look at the cost of advertising, or even good-quality brochures, and in any case we have no budget for that sort of thing.'*
Chances are that you are already investing heavily in the things that will be most important to your B2B or service brand's definition – your people, your technology, your processes. A B2B brand operating in a market where all the major customers are known can easily dispense with the multi-million-pound promotional budget.

Remembering that brand strength and brand loyalty result from the level of interactivity between brand and customer, many a B2B or service brand should have a fabulous opportunity to build a strong and valuable brand. That they so often miss this opportunity is down either to their denial of branding, or , ironically, to an excess of '*surface fluff*' branding – the failure to follow through the claims of the brand into the substance of the product.

A financial services provider has a huge opportunity for multiple contacts and complex customer associations, but having first ignored brands as irrelevant, some now have turned to branding by logo and slogan. Unfortunately the use of engaging associations, whether it be with black horses or the sponsorship of *Frasier* on Channel 4, all too often comes to nothing in the reality of the experience. Queuing through your lunch break doesn't gel with images of freedom, nor does having your branch closed and being forced through a call centre that is always '*experiencing particularly high call levels*'. And a collapsing pension fund isn't funny. If a JD Wetherspoon pub or club advertised great nights out for young adults, only to provide bingo, dominoes and the occasional beetle drive, the effect would not be dissimilar.

The brand as evidence of appropriate performance

While each of the definitions of a brand so far discussed can be applied to a service or B2B brand, perhaps we also need a definition that focuses on the customer's expectations of performance and the appropriateness of the supplier's response to those expectations.

Figure 7.1 lists some of the most typical requirements from B2B and service suppliers, and so some of the most typical bases on which to build a brand definition. To some degree these bases increase in significance (rather like the emotional charge model) and so we might expect higher levels of loyalty at the upper end.

Some important riders should be attached to this list:

1. It is indicative only of typical expectations, not a complete list.
2. Rarely does a customer expect all of this, and still less would they get it, but nor are they mutually exclusive requirements.

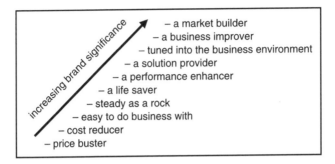

Figure 7.1 *B2B brand performance expectations and rising brand significance*

A brand may form its definition around an almost endless variety of mixes and matches.

3. As ever in marketing, brands must target market segments comprising customers with similar requirements and attitudes. Choosing the definition depends of course on the dominant expectations of the target segment.

4. Expectations change as markets change.

Price busters and cost reducers

New entrants to a market have often donned the price buster mantle, or its more sophisticated elder sibling, the cost reducer. It is also an approach taken by brands trying to shake up a long-established market with incumbent brands dozing quietly.

Companies offering business training through the internet have tended to lead with claims of cost reduction, a brand definition that they can often substantiate with some ease. Moving up to the level of performance enhancer or business improver (brand platforms occupied by many of their more traditional competitors) will present a much harder challenge if it is to be substantiated with any conviction.

Easy to do business with

American Express takes all the effort out of corporate business travel. The Amex 'in-plant' is a common feature of many a large business, taking on all the tasks short of making the trips themselves. This 'easy to do business with' brand now has to take on the challenge of those managers who think the internet makes it easier for them to do it themselves. The fact that Amex might be better tuned into the business environment may just give it the edge.

This example demonstrates two important principles of this model of the brand as evidence of appropriate performance. First, meeting more than one expectation can often make for a stronger brand, provided you don't get greedy and try to claim too much. Second, like the emotional charge model, greater brand strength with its attendant enhanced loyalty tends to result from meeting the higher level expectations.

Steady as a rock

The Tetra Brik is a good example of a brand that is 'steady as a rock'. Its numerous users, often creating new markets made possible by the packaging technology, depend on the absolute reliability of the brand. And if things *do* go wrong, then they depend on the ability of the brand to put them right. Tetra Brik has much at stake if its product fails the customer, and the customer knows that, and so a strong bond of common interest is forged between supplier, customer and consumer.

Lifesavers

DHL works hard to define its brand around reliability and speed. Driven by the business world's need to do things fast, and globally, DHL represents a 'lifesaver' brand. Just hearing the letters DHL brings a sigh of relief – not a bad emotional response to associate with your brand. And then along comes e-mail. Now there is less need for such heroics – huge documents can be sent in seconds with no need for planes, boats and trains. The DHL brand must change into something more than a specialist emergency service. Perhaps a provider of wider business solutions that recognise the changing demands of truly global businesses?

Tuned-in performance enhancers, solution providers, business improvers and market builders

If a consumer brand must tune into social and life values, so a B2B brand must tune into the commercial environment of the time. The Intel brand captured the loyalty of PC manufacturers for a variety of reasons, not least because the brand was both a performance enhancer through the ever-increasing speed of its ever-diminishing chips, and a market builder through its consumer franchise. Times change and the PC builders are becoming more interested in cost reduction in a maturing, not to say saturated, market. Should Intel take its brand down a price buster road, perhaps with its high-volume Celeron microprocessor line, or does it stick to its market builder definition by encouraging the development of software applications that will demand its high-speed capabilities? The launch of the Pentium III Xeon microprocessor, specifically designed to improve the performance of large websites and e-business applications, fitted the latter direction. Which would you choose?

The B2B brand with the consumer franchise: a class act

There is a class of B2B brand that manages to operate at a number of the higher levels of customer expectation, while also matching the expectations of their customers' customers. This is the brand with its own consumer franchise, like Lycra and Teflon from DuPont, or Nutrasweet from Monsanto, or Gore-Tex, or the Intel Pentium 4.

Such brands clearly enhance their customers' performance; they help to improve their business performance, but most importantly they also help to build the market for those customers. The big brands in the sports clothing market have much to thank Lycra for, just as the big PC brands owe a debt to the 'Intel inside'.

These brands have a triple value – for the owner, for the B2B customer, and for the consumer. The value does not come cheaply; the creation of a consumer franchise takes heavy investment in communication strategies, like the famous Nutrasweet gumball campaign where millions of gumballs were mailed to consumers to demonstrate the effectiveness and natural taste of the product. Such brands have to manage two sets of customers – the end consumer and the manufacturer that uses their product.

8

Valuing the brand – not just for the accountants

It is clear that brands are hugely valuable properties that will have received significant investment over time. Not so very long ago, brand managers may have been inclined to talk of the 'inestimable value' of their brand. Of course, they meant this in praise of its undeniable, but immeasurable value, but no longer should they take such a trusting and accepting view.

In 1985, Reckitt & Colman bought Airwick from Ciba-Geigy, with a good chunk of the payment being for 'goodwill', the accountant's term for the value of such apparently indefinable things as Airwick's customers, and its brand. In fact, 'goodwill' makes these items quite definable, placing an actual market value on them. The normal accounting practice would have been for Reckitt & Colman to pay the money but see no increase in the net assets shown on the balance sheet. Not a new problem, but Reckitt & Colman had a new solution – it decided to capitalise the value of the brand.

In 1987, Grand Met bought Heublein, owners of the Smirnoff brand. Grand Met announced that it would include £588 million on its balance sheet for acquired brands.

These two moves were unusual, but not revolutionary, Reckitt & Colman and Grand Met were only valuing acquired brands as part of the complexity of acquisitions and valuations. The real revolution came in 1988 when Philip Morris paid $12.9 billion for the Kraft food company, a sum that was four times the book value of the tangible assets in the business. What Philip Morris was really paying for was the intangible assets of the brands.

In the same year, RHM decided to value all its brands, not just newly acquired ones, and after much debate in learned journals many more have followed its example. Brand managers now have an additional responsibility. As well as building the value of the brand in the customer's eyes they now must also please the accountants. The problem has become how to value the brand and as yet there is no one agreed method.

The task was relatively easy when a company was buying a brand as part of an acquisition – what it paid was what it thought it was worth, the market decided. But what if you already owned it? Three methods stand out from the crowd:

▒ **The Existing Use method.** This attempts to value the brand based on the price premium it receives over its generic competition, plus a calculation for the level of recognition the brand has in the market and the esteem in which customers hold the brand.

▒ **The Earnings Multiple system.** This calculates something called brand earnings, largely based on the cash flow provided by the brand, and multiplies that by a figure based on brand strength. Brand strength is a combination of factors including market share, global presence, investment, and any brand protection measures taken.

▒ **The Interbrand system** (as developed by the firm of that name). Recent profitability is multiplied by a number between 1 and 20 that represents a balance of seven important aspects of the brand:
  – its leadership position;
  – its likely longevity;

- the stability of the market in which it operates;
- its globality;
- its future trend;
- the level of marketing support;
- its legal protection.

Each of these allows a good deal of room for subjective analysis, but as the practice becomes more common so do the standards used for this kind of analysis.

Implications for brand management

The 'how to' of brand valuation need not detain us longer, but what about the impact of brand valuations on the role of the brand manager? Brand valuation is a discipline that forces the brand manager to focus on some rather important issues:

▪ What actually represents strength and value in our business – is it the brands?
▪ What is the relative importance of our brands compared to, let's say, our physical assets?
▪ If a brand has a value, then it can be sold. What will be best for the business, selling a brand or continuing to invest in it?
▪ Valuing brands helps puts a price on licensing and royalties.
▪ The value of a brand is not based solely on today's receipts but, as for any investment, also on tomorrow's potential. The practice of valuing brands forces the business to regard those brands as investments over time, making quite clear the brand manager's responsibility to build and sustain that investment, consistently. (Remember this argument the next time the boss asks for a cut in the advertising budget!)
▪ Is the practice of branding more profitable than simply selling products and services?

Branding and profitability

The last of these issues deserves some more attention, simply because it turns out to be good news in the main. Strong brands tend to be more profitable than weak ones.

Research by PIMS (Profit Impact of Market Strategies) shows that in the UK food market the No 1 food brand in any particular sector has an average profit margin of 18 per cent while the No 2 brand has an average of only 4 per cent. Remember that these are averages – many No 2 brands run at a loss. Not surprisingly, a good number of these No 2 brands have withdrawn from the game.

These figures suggest that in the food business at least, it is not branding per se that is profitable, but successful branding, and in this market that means being the brand leader. In other markets, there is still room for a multiplicity of brands, but being the biggest often helps.

Table 8.1 shows the average return on investment (ROI) assessed across 3,000 diverse UK businesses, looking at how they stood based on market share (brand strength) and quality.

These figures alone are by no means conclusive but they suggest some truths that other pieces of evidence would give backing to – investing in brands to gain market share is as rewarding as investing in the product to improve quality, and if a good-quality product also has a good brand standing, then it will be even more likely to return good profits. Strong brands tend to return good profits for a variety of reasons:

■ Top brands command premium prices.
■ Winning new customers is easier and so less costly.

Table 8.1 PIMS research on brands and ROI

	Low quality	Medium quality	High quality
High market share	21.00	25.00	38.00
Medium market share	14.00	20.00	27.00
Low market share	7.00	13.00	20.00

- Good brands win customer loyalty, and loyal customers will cost less to retain and service.
- A strong brand gives negotiating power to the supplier.
- High market share gives you presence in the market, and that brings knowledge, and that allows vision, and that facilitates an ability to change (but only if you choose to learn).
- A good brand evidences a unique match between company capabilities and market needs – a good brand is therefore an expression of competitive advantage.

Brand management – the strategy

Brands don't come first. If they do, then you have the prospect of muddle at best, with incoherence and chaos the more likely result. If we remember the level of investment put into brands, then imagine the waste that can result from asking them to work in a business structure or culture that doesn't suit. Sometimes a successful brand in the wrong place can be as damaging as a flop; it can work as a brake to the business progressing in its chosen direction. Business strategy must come first, and brands must fit within that context. For the world's leading brands, brand management takes place in the boardroom.

Part II takes us through a process for the development and positioning of brands within the context of your business strategy. Not entirely chronological; a lot must go on at once, and of course, if your brands exist already, you may need to do some backtracking.

The process, illustrated in Figure PII.1, sees a continual narrowing of the brand's focus, funnelling down from the broad positioning based on the business strategy to the specific positioning based on benefits that establish a definition of value. This positioning is 'experienced' by the customer through a number of 'brand interactions'.

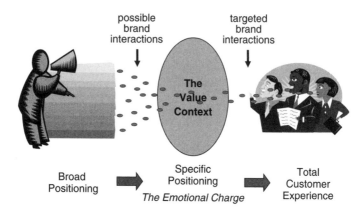

Figure PII.1 *The brand positioning process*

9

Business strategy – the brand in context

In theory, defining the business strategy should come first, followed by the creation of the brands and the brand architecture to support that strategy. In reality, companies often have an existing portfolio of brands and find themselves scouting around for things to do with them. They are the 'proud' owners of excellent brands, but ones that can't be made to work within their strategy.

Strategies for razor blades and pens

Gillette has long prospered with razors and blades, applying 'high-tech' innovations to global brands, but a business model that works for these brands has not worked so well with Parker, Papermate or Waterman, famous and worthy brands of pens that might prosper more in other hands...

The understanding of business strategy, and so the demands placed on the brand manager, might be simplified into the answers to two questions: 1) how do we intend to grow, and what level of risk might that involve? and 2) what values will drive our business? By answering these questions, and seeking to match the brand strategy to the business strategy, the brand manager will have arrived at what we will call the *broad positioning* of the brand. This will be our starting point for brand positioning in Chapter 11.

Growth, branding and risk management: the brand halo

Business growth is a risky thing, particularly if that growth takes you off your home turf. If your growth activities simply involve doing more of what you already do (*market penetration*), then the risk is much less than for launching new products, entering new markets or diversifying. These levels of risk are illustrated in Figure 9.1, the Ansoff Matrix. The percentage figures indicate the comparative likelihood of success for each strategy.

Risk is necessary in business, but managed risk is usually best, and brands provide an excellent means of managing the

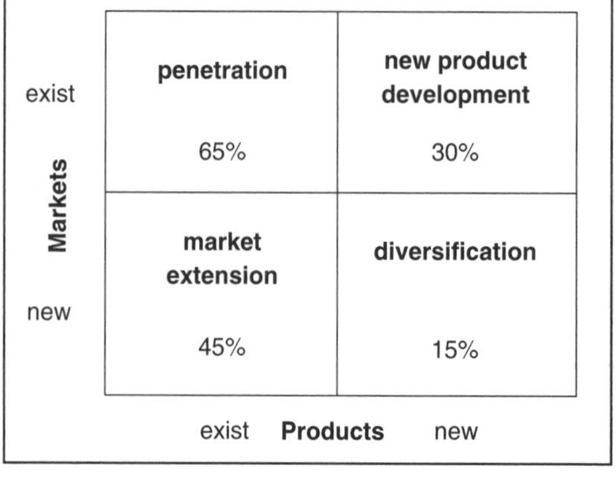

	penetration 65%	new product development 30%
Markets (exist / new)	market extension 45%	diversification 15%

exist **Products** new

Figure 9.1 *Understanding risk: the Ansoff Matrix*

risks involved in growth strategies beyond market penetration. A successful brand can act like a protective halo to be put around the more risky of your growth activities. It can also lead you into foolish and lazy actions – relying on the *halo effect* can work for good or ill.

New product development

The hugely successful launch of the Mars ice cream bar created an entirely new market worth millions, but that success was due to the healthy existence and protective halo of the original Mars Bar brand. Would the launch of a Tunnock's ice cream bar (Tunnock's is a thoroughly splendid but rather low-profile chocolate wafer biscuit) have made as big a splash?

Each time Kellogg's launches a new breakfast cereal, it rides in on the back of its Kellogg's name, acting as a 'validated identity brand' (see Chapter 13) and providing a protective halo. The new trial rate by consumers is guaranteed to be higher because of the Kellogg's name, and the chance of getting it on to the supermarket shelf is increased (though never assured).

While FMCG and retail may provide the high-profile examples, it is perhaps in the B2B and industrial branding area that the halo effect can be of greatest value. Launching new products is hard work if it relies principally on a physical sales effort rather than a high-profile media campaign. Getting the customer to give you the time to present your ideas is not easy, even if they are a regular contact – today's emergencies tend to squeeze out discussions on tomorrow's opportunities. A strong brand doesn't guarantee a hearing, but it makes it more likely, and broadens the base of those who might want to hear. So often in B2B relationships it is the breadth of contacts that is vital to success, and the brand halo can help you to extend your reach.

Diversifying for growth

Virgin

Almost every step along Virgin's growth path has been diversification – from record label to airline, to hotelier, to cola producer, to financial services provider, to train company, and so it goes on. Virgin is very clear what it must do to reduce the enormous risks inherent in these ventures. It conducts more market research than most businesses would think necessary, it makes use of expert partners, in particular its suppliers, and it makes full use of the Virgin brand halo. Its ability to transfer the values behind the brand name to each of its diversified ventures is a role model for any company seeking to use a corporate brand to support and manage the risk of an ambitious growth strategy (see Chapter 13).

Diversifying to escape decline

A rather more challenging use of a brand is seen when a business chooses to diversify in order to escape decline.

Marlboro

Philip Morris, owner of the Marlboro brand, envisages a slow decline of that brand as a result of increasing restrictions on tobacco advertising. This is not a situation that it is about to take lying down, not least because the brand is one of its most important assets, valued at $23 billion. Plans under consideration include diversification into hotels and leisure, under the Marlboro brand. It hopes that the halo effect will ease its path into this highly competitive market. But there are some mighty big challenges. Can the Marlboro brand values be translated to a hotel? Presumably guests will still be urged not to smoke in bed? Might it be that this particular brand halo will prove to be an obstacle rather than an assistance? Some argue that a better use of its assets would be to milk Marlboro as it declines and invest the funds in growth strategies for other established brands in the portfolio, such as Kraft or Miller.

Entering new markets

This is fertile ground for horror stories, particularly where brand managers have an over-inflated conception of the power of their brand halo, or are just plain lazy.

Ben and Jerry's

Ben and Jerry's ice cream was a phenomenal success in the United States with its quirky mix of showmanship, fun, local referencing, entrepreneurial spirit and social conscience, a formula and definition that meant very little when the brand was launched in the United Kingdom. Not only did UK consumers care little for the plight of Vermont dairy farmers (the brand's support of this beleaguered group in the United States won it a warm following), but few of them got the jokes behind ice cream names such as Cherry Garcia.

Imagining that you have a protective brand halo when either nobody has heard of you, or is confused by your brand definition, or has a different conception of what it stands for, can be an arresting experience.

Branding and value drivers – defining the brand

A value driver is a set of ideas or principles, embedded in the company's culture, which allows all members of the business to identify what their contribution is to overall success. It is what makes the business tick, or better, what makes it hum.

Michael Treacy and Fred Wiersema, in their book *The Discipline of Market Leaders* (HarperCollins), identified three value drivers that provide an excellent model for identifying and implementing a business strategy:

▓ operational excellence;
▓ product leadership;
▓ customer intimacy.

All three may be present in any successful business, but for a *really* successful business, one or other of these drivers will stand out, distinguishing the business for its staff and its customers, and distinguishing it from its competitors.

The brand managers may choose to represent to their customers, through the brand, the key driver in their business. The advantage of this is the ability to communicate the brand's role as representing the unique match between customers' needs and suppliers' capabilities. Confusion of drivers can lead to confusion of brand definition.

Operational excellence is about doing what you do, well. The cogs of your processes are well oiled. Such 'excellence' can bring significant competitive advantage, in a market where reliability and consistency is important, or prices are competitive.

IKEA

IKEA is driven by operational excellence, achieving huge efficiencies through its logistics chain, from manufacturer to store, and its in-store 'self-selection, self-collection' formula. The IKEA brand makes a virtue of these internal processes, shouting out the excellent value it can provide for its customers (just witness how many first-time house buyers on a shoestring budget kit out their home at IKEA).

A service provider driven by operational excellence would perhaps have a no frills brand that spoke of low costs resulting from the experience and economy of the supplier. EasyJet communicates its key driver through the brand in this way.

Product leadership is about producing the best, or the market dominant products. Businesses with high rates of innovation and patent application often have this value at their heart. It is hard to imagine a successful pharmaceuticals company that is not driven by this value. It must always be at the leading edge, pushing at the boundaries and, most importantly, be seen to be doing so. The brand definition of such businesses will be appropriately innovative and entrepreneurial.

Microsoft

The pace of innovation achieved by Microsoft is amazing, the downside being that you can sometimes feel out of date as soon as you carry its latest product out of the store (which puts me way out of date: rephrase that last comment – as you download their latest product…). The Microsoft brand represents innovation and state of the art, and is perhaps happy that it also represents a small element of risk. Brands that push at the boundaries will occasionally make mistakes; it's almost expected by the customer. When there are doubts (and much publicity) about a new version of Windows, sales just keep on rising. It would seem that a lot of us want to be part of that leading edge, bugs and all.

Customer intimacy is the desire and the ability to identify with specific customer needs, and to match products and services accordingly. What distinguishes the customer-intimate business is its stated determination to develop close customer relationships, and to act on the resultant knowledge at all levels of its operation. It will probably have a wide menu of products and services, and the ability to mix and match these to suit individual customer requirements – or perhaps it will go further than this and offer a totally bespoke service.

Many B2B and service brands will aim to put this value at the heart of their brand definition. The upside is that it enables them to project an image of personalised service. A potential downside could be that an apparent claim to be able to do anything is non-credible. This requires careful brand management. The customer-intimate driver should not lead you down an unfocused road. Rather, think of it as intimacy within clearly defined boundaries, boundaries set as a result of your business strategy and your approach to market segmentation (see Chapter 10).

Quest International

Quest International supplies fragrances to the perfume industry. Each of its customers' products is unique, and the fragrance is equally unique – there are no off-the-shelf solutions in this business. The perfumer's art is as much one of black magic as chemistry and this makes for very demanding, and often seemingly eccentric, customers. Quest must be able to identify with this, but, more than that, ensure that its own people can work on this basis. Customer intimacy is essential for success, resulting in an absolute identification with the customer's needs, and the ability to focus the whole organistion on meeting them. The brand represents that ability.

10

Segmentation – a source of competitive advantage

A brand helps you to target your audience. A learning brand gets to know its customers, and goes out looking for them. Segmentation is the process of identifying those target audiences and understanding them in such depth that the offer, through the brand, can be tailored with both precision and sufficient uniqueness to win competitive advantage.

Other books deal with the mechanics of segmentation. Here we will focus on the importance of segmentation to the development of a winning brand strategy and, in particular, the need to practise segmentation with a level of sophistication greater than the norm.

Definitions and purpose: avoiding the 'me too' scenario

A segment is a group of people with similar needs, perceptions, attitudes and behaviours, concerning your offer and offers like yours. In theory the process of segmentation could break these groups down into micro-segments, or even down to unique individuals. How far you need to go depends on the nature of your market, and your intentions and ability to vary your offer.

For most consumer goods, the segments come in tens if not hundreds of thousands of consumers. For a B2B supplier the entire customer base may only number 100, and segments comprising single figures may be appropriate.

Whatever the scale, the intention remains the same: to develop an offer that meets the needs of the segment as uniquely as possible. One of the problems for the brand manager is that if your basis of segmentation is the same as your competitors', in other words you are all targeting the same people with the same needs, then the opportunities for uniqueness are somewhat limited. The brand name may be the only point of difference. While this is of course a key purpose of the brand – to find differentiation in crowded markets – it might be better to find a more novel way of segmenting the market in the first place. Very often it will require only a small shift in your view to find potential competitive advantage staring you in the face.

Choices

The thing about segmentation is that there are always choices, and it is important to try to find a choice not already taken by a competitor.

Kellogg's and Weetabix

In the breakfast cereal market, Kellogg's has chosen to place individual brands in all of the available segments, from health to fun, diet control to energy, traditional to novelty. Its promotional spend is consequently huge (£55 million in the United Kingdom) but it occupies 8 out of the top 10 positions for breakfast cereal brands sold in the United Kingdom.

Weetabix makes another choice: to focus on fewer segments through far fewer brands. Weetabix is number two in the United Kingdom's top 10 selling breakfast cereal brands, with a promotional spend of £15 million focused on a product once described as 'a dour, sugarless flaked wheat block that looks like it was designed by the Soviet Cereal Secretariat in 1951'. In fact, Weetabix is the SAS of the breakfast cereal market compared to the Kellogg's Red Army.

The brand as focus for the marketing mix

Having identified the segment, and understood its dynamics, the marketer will need to construct an offer based on the four Ps – product, price, promotion and place. The brand is the focus that puts this 'marketing mix' to work. Not only do the four Ps interact with each other, they must balance with each other for a successful mix. New brand launches are particularly prone to misfits in the mix.

Babycham

When Babycham was first launched, the product, promotion and place were well thought out, but the price was too low. This was a drink ('fake' champagne) that men bought for their girlfriends to impress them (remember, this was the 1960s!). But at such a low price who was going to be impressed? The product was relaunched at a suitably ego-enhancing price and remains one of the brand icons of a now very different world.

Different mix, different brand?

Since a segment is a group with unique needs it is quite possible that different segments will require sufficiently different market mixes to warrant different brands.

ICI Dulux

In the market for decorative paint used by professional tradesmen, ICI Dulux found itself targeting two key, but quite different segments – the small firms of decorators and the major contractor firms. Table 10.1 shows some of the bases on which the segments were compared, and found to be so different as to require two separate brands, Dulux Trade and Glidden.

When it looked at buying behaviour in particular, it found that the brand loyalty of self-employed professional decorators and the influence of their clients (brand-aware houseowners) made the use of the Dulux brand a must. The buyer for the major contractor demanded cost reductions that would have compromised the main brand had it attempted to work in both segments A new brand was the perfect solution, and one already existed in the ICI world group – Glidden is the main ICI paint brand in the United States.

Table 10.1　Segmentation and branding in the professional paint market

Base	Major Contractor	Small Decorator Firm
Size of firm	200+	1–5
Size of purchase	Industrial scale, larger pack size	Domestic scale, smaller pack size
Specification	Professional	from client, usually a homeowner
Distribution channel	Direct from supplier	Builders or decorators' merchant
Purchasing function	Professional buyer direct to supplier	Owner/manager through merchant
Lead influence on purchase decision	Price and cost analysis	Client specification and brand loyalty
Brand	Glidden	Dulux Trade

Novel segmentation

There may be some fairly obvious ways to segment a market but the problem with these 'easy options' is that your competitors are probably seeing things just the same, and where's the competitive advantage in that? The pursuit of novel ways to segment will often unearth new understanding of the dynamics of the marketplace and gain you significant competitive advantage.

Branding in a mature 'no brand' market

Segmentation of the fertiliser market

A fertiliser manufacturer found its product to be in slow decline in a mature market. It decided to segment as a means of finding new offers, testing first the more obvious 'cuts': crop type, geography, seasonality, all used by its competitors to different degrees. Finally it hit on a simple truth – wheat didn't buy fertiliser, and nor did East Anglia, it was farmers every time! Farmers came from different backgrounds, with widely differing attitudes, aspirations and buying behaviours. Once the manufacturer started to explore these factors, it began to understand (almost for the first time) what really made people buy its product. The final segmentation was based on attitudes and needs, the traditional family farmer for instance having a rather different outlook as compared with the graduate of an agricultural college managing a large estate.

Division of the market into six segments allowed the business to focus on six different marketing mixes, each manifested in a carefully honed brand proposition. It was able to add more relevant value, remove irrelevant activities or costs, achieve greater brand loyalty, better prices, increased share, and improved profitability. All of this in a market that was seen as hugely mature and no place for branding...

Escaping from the A1, B2 syndrome

In consumer markets the slicing of segments by A1, B2-style socio-economic demographics has been worked to death – the methodology of the new millennium is 'psychographics'.

Dulux and the DIY market

Having discussed the Dulux brand in the professional market, let's turn to the DIY market, where the brand has proved to be one of the most enduring, largely through its ability to evolve. The process of evolution has been managed to a great extent through a continual updating of the basis of segmentation.

In the 1960s the boom in DIY was based on a raft of new, easier-to-use products – the era of Formica and Fablon. Dulux adopted a segmentation based on application needs, and developed sub-brands accordingly, such as Dulux Weathershield for outside walls.

Into the 1970s and attitudes were changing. DIY was an established norm and consumers were seeking more. They didn't just want to protect their homes, they wanted to transform them. Dulux became an aspirational brand and new segmentation was required. Terms such as planners and appliers evolved, and soon became segments, each needing their own marketing mix and brand treatment.

The more demanding 1980s and 1990s saw consumers seeking increasing personalisation of their homes. The 'nesting' culture (an updated form of the Englishman's home being his castle, where a desire for personal and private spaces strongly influences attitudes and behaviours) called for another look at segmentation – planners were not just planners any more. Figure 10.1 gives a diagrammatic description of a new approach to segmentation using psychographic terminology.

Different slices of this spectrum can be targeted by sub-brands – 'Dulux Satinwood' for the finish fanatic, 'Dulux KidsZone' for the adventurous 'colour crazies'.

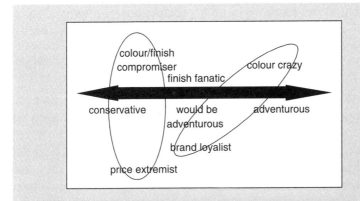

Figure 10.1 *Psychographic segmentation for decorative paint*

Micro-segmentation – anti-segmentation?

The revolution in IT has meant that, in theory, brands should be able to target segments as small as an individual. In practice, where does this leave brands? Will they become so personalised that you make it up yourself? Will brands become very much more targeted, or will they expand to become wider umbrellas representing 'lifestyles' within which personalised choices are made? In practice, the mass market brands must still target mass markets, but they can always make it seem that they are being more attentive to the individual...

A Barclays poster campaign introduces 'the Sarah loan', and 'the Nigel loan', suggesting that it is able to cater for segments as small as an individual. What it means is there will be a menu of choices, but it is an advance on the old days of one size fits all.

The Mercedes 'whoever you are' campaign appears to target every segment and every personality. Using some well-worn stereotypes, it makes it seem that anyone can find their ideal car from within a Mercedes range that has grown only marginally.

Rather than an exercise in micro-segmentation, this is more a case of a traditional mass-market segmentation research study being shouted out loud from the page and the screen.

HSBC's 'different people, one bank' campaign suggests either an abandonment of segmentation – one size fits all – or, like Barclays, a claim that the bank is so flexible that it can cater for any and all varieties. In truth, few brands have managed to move from traditional segmentation models, despite the overload (or perhaps because of the overload) of information available through electronic transactions, largely because they are still the products of business models based on mass production and uniformity. The opportunity for the genuinely tailored brand is still there to be seized, but only by someone who can escape the traditional business models of the 20th century. This is, perhaps, the realm of the internet brand, but as yet we are more conscious of the failures than the successes. Too many internet brands have been based on business models of no real substance – still a recipe for brand failure.

11

Brand positioning – securing a place in the customer's mind

Brand positioning is more than just stating your case. Plenty of people can come up with a brand definition and place it on the market, but then plenty of brands wither and die. Successful long-term brands must be able to find, or create, a relevant space in the target customer's mind, and cement their brand's definition and values there. Then, as minds change, so must the brands.

The process of brand positioning is intended to identify and target those spaces in the customer's mind. The process of cementing your brand's definition there will be dealt with in Part III. Positioning isn't easy; there are all sorts of wrong positionings awaiting you:

- **Underpositioning,** where you stand for nothing in particular, occupying no space in the customer's mind, and giving them no reason to buy, or even care.
- **Overpositioning,** where you are so narrowly specific that once the handful of target customers has bought, you're done.
- **Confused positioning,** where you're just trying to be too many things at once and contradictions and conflicts

abound. (Does the hugely successful KitKat break the rules of positioning – is it a biscuit, a sweet, a snack, a treat... ?)

▓ **Irrelevant positioning** – so your brand will help remove the stains *inside* my radiators without my having to close them down... who cares?

▓ **Doubtful positioning,** making claims that nobody believes and only the most gullible will become your customers – not a good recipe for building sales by word of mouth...

And then after all of this come the risks, the pain and the expense of repositioning. Sometimes there is a happy ending...

The Marlboro image

Marlboro, one of the earliest filter-tip cigarettes, was originally positioned to appeal to women, and failing to make great headway there it tried to target men, among whom its filter tip was considered positively 'sissy'... Marlboro adopted a cowboy as an image and repositioned the brand as the 'he-man's smoke'. The rest we know.

Boldly going...

Usually, a brand must try to avoid a 'middle of the road' positioning, but taking any kind of extreme stance inevitably means that some will disapprove. The Benetton campaign of the 1990s is an example of such positioning, but many have 'learnt' from the success of that brand. A sense of disapproval has now become an important facet of some brands; creating as it does an 'in crowd' feel for those who *do* approve. Nowhere is this seen more than when establishing a new brand. Häagen-Dazs was launched against a backdrop of ice cream being for kids, and wanted to escape these kinds of associations. The brand was shown with adult interactions, sometimes with provocative images that could only bring disapproval from some, but helped establish a loyalty from those specifically targeted. (Getting the market segmentation right is essential for such a strategy.)

Some brands even manage to play cleverly on their realisation that not everyone likes them. Marmite sought to position its unique taste by recognising that some folk just can't stand the stuff – '*I Hate*' Marmite posters ran alongside the '*My Mate*' posters in its advertising campaign.

The process

The following process, adapted from Philip Kotler, aims to help you avoid these expensive mistakes. It is a broad process allowing plenty of scope for variations on a theme:

1. Establish the *broad positioning*, as it forms from your business strategy.
2. For each target market or segment, develop the *specific positioning*, probably based on a clearly defined list of benefits, both tangible and intangible (don't forget the *emotional charge!*).
3. Identify the *value context* of the brand.
4. Develop the intended *total customer experience*.

Figure 11.1 illustrates the process as a series of refinements that enable the brand to target the final customer with great precision. First comes a funnelling activity, moving from *broad positioning* (step 1) to *specific positioning* based on benefits (step 2).

Then this specific positioning is placed in a particular *value context* (step 3) – what is the customer getting, and for how much? The value context is represented by the portion of the oval through which the brand's specific positioning passes – in this case, we might read this as '*getting more for the same*'. '*Getting more for more*' would perhaps be the top slice (see step 3 on page 83). The manifestation of all this is seen in the range of interactions the customer has with the brand, the whole forming what I have called the *total customer experience* (step 4).

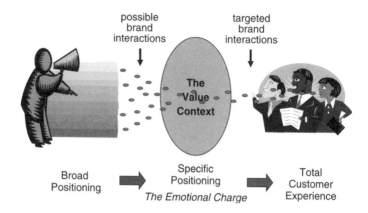

Figure 11.1 *The brand positioning process*

Crudely speaking, the more of these planned interactions that hit their target, and stick, the greater the customer's experience and so the stronger and more meaningful the brand. If the brand manager is working with the idea of 'shooting' these interactions *at* the customer, then this might indicate that the brand has a high need to *push* its attentions on to the customer, typical perhaps of a brand with a relatively low emotional charge. A brand with a higher emotional charge might expect the customer to engage more voluntarily, and the resultant interactions might be more akin to an *envelopment* of the customer rather than an assault on their person.

1. Broad positioning

Your business strategy (Chapter 9) will have generated a broad positioning based on three factors:

■ your growth strategy and the demands that places on your brands;
■ your value drivers;
■ the brand architecture best suited to achieve your business strategy (see Chapter 13).

2. Specific positioning

Good segmentation (see Chapter 10) will give you a deep understanding of your customer's needs, attitudes and behaviours. Matching these with your own capabilities (see Chapter 5) will help you select the specific benefits that make up your offer. This will be your specific positioning – the value given to the customer, the representation of your leading capabilities, and your basis for competitive advantage.

To some degree the number of benefits identified will depend on the number of segments that the brand is targeting. In general, the greater the number of benefits argued, the more diffused the brand definition becomes. While this might allow the brand to work across many segments, it will also tend to leave it open to competition that might take a more single-minded approach.

Aquafresh

Some brands focus on just one benefit, so maximising their impact and their credibility. Others manage a range of benefits. The Aquafresh brand of toothpaste selects three: protection, whiteness and fresh breath. The red, white and blue bands in the toothpaste help it to communicate these benefits even at the point of use – a valuable customer interaction.

Potential sources for specific positioning

Each of the definitions of a brand discussed in Part I can provide the basis for a specific brand positioning:

- the *emotional charge* of the brand, whether that rests in authenticity, performance, satisfaction in use or social expression;
- the *personality* of the brand, whether it is male or female, young or old, cool or dynamic, hip or hop;

■ the level of *loyalty* to be expected, whether it will be promiscuous, passive or passionate;

■ the *unique match* forged between the company capabilities and the needs of the customer – a particularly fruitful area for the B2B and service brand, and closely related to the last of these sources;

■ the *evidence of appropriate performance* – matching the value drivers.

Value drivers – in the eye of the beholder

In a B2B or service industry it may be useful to look again at a model already used in establishing the brand's broad positioning – Treacy and Wiersema's value drivers. This time it will be viewed from the customer's perspective – what is *their* leading driver and so what type of brand response is required? In effect, we are using this model to find a match between the supplier's strategy and the customer's strategy.

If the customer is driven by *operational excellence* then issues such as consistency and reliability, cost reduction, process re-engineering and the like will come to the fore. If they are driven by *product leadership* then they might be looking for innovation, the ability to help with and speed new product development, and an entrepreneurial attitude to risk. The customers led by *intimacy* with their own customers may seek suppliers that will help them achieve the flexibility required of such an approach.

It will be seen that the lead drivers of supplier and customer do not have to be the same; indeed, a customer driven by operational excellence might be best served working with a supplier driven by product leadership, if that product leadership was in areas that would help increase the customer's own efficiencies. Similarly, a customer driven by product leadership might seek out a supplier with an abundance of customer intimacy in order to gain the necessary responsiveness and flexibility.

Narrowing the benefits field...

As the specific positioning emerges from these sources it can be fine-tuned by looking for particular benefits in the following sources:

■ **Particular attributes** – specific claims about the brand, such as the Australian fruit juice Berri that makes much of the fact that it is '*100% Australian owned*'. This might also include claims to a particular heritage – the oldest brand, the most traditional brand, the brand still using the original methods (an approach beloved of malt whiskies).

Of course, such attributes are essentially features of the product and as such could be thought of as rather weak, but features can be turned into benefits provided they can be linked to a distinct customer need – does the malt whisky drinker feel better for thinking his dram is 'traditional' rather than modern?

■ **Specific user benefits** – the safety of a Volvo, the ease of a Flymo, the versatility of a Black & Decker Workmate.

■ **Focus on specific users** – the Apple Mac for graphic designers, Peoplesoft for HR managers, the Xai brand of football boots – it makes no other sports footwear, so marking itself out as a specialist, not a fashion icon (though of course it hopes to become just that among footballers).

■ **Benefits of heritage** – the Hovis brand reassures us with '*it's as good for you today as it's always been*'.

■ **Reference to the competition** – Avis '*tries harder*', Duracell '*lasts longer*', the Pepsi taste challenge.

■ **Status in the category** – Kodak *is* film, Xerox *is* copiers, or the AA as the '*fourth emergency service*'. An interesting twist on this is the '*No FT, no comment*' campaign, a clear statement of the newspaper's status in the category, but also a clever reference to a common feeling of guilt among its target audience – another kind of emotional charge.

Perceptual mapping – occupying a space in the customer's mind

A valuable tool in identifying the brand's specific positioning is the perceptual map. An example is shown in Figure 11.2.

Such maps seek to position the brand by using two (or more) factors considered to be important in the purchasing process. As the tool's name suggests, it is the customer's real perceptions that count, not your own beliefs or assertions. Using this tool calls for a high degree of honesty and detachment on the brand manager's part. The tool can be used in a number of ways.

First, through research, it can be used to understand where target customers place your proposition *in their mind*, and relative to other offers, and to compare that with your intended proposition and positioning.

A second use might be to plot the competition against various mixes of factors and to look for any 'gaps' in the map. Such gaps may be opportunities for you to establish a unique position. BMW was arguably the first manufacturer to position a middle-price, mid-sized, high-performance car, exploiting a gap that had stood open between the likes of Ford on the one hand and Porsche or Ferrari on the other. Ford's attempts to compete

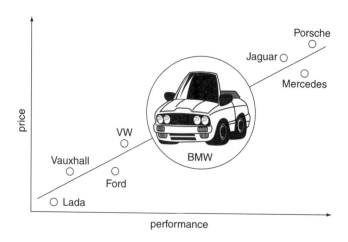

Figure 11.2 *A perceptual map for brands of motor car*

in earnest in this newly identified segment had to wait for its purchase of the Jaguar brand.

A third, and perhaps most significant use in terms of specific positioning, is to assess the wide variety of factors that impact on the purchase decision and to see which particular combinations will allow your brand the most competitive advantage, while being of genuine importance to the customer. If these factors can be effectively communicated to the customer (in essence telling them what they *really* want), then the brand's positioning on this basis will have a high chance of succeeding. Such an approach does, however, require great subtlety. Customers, and particularly professional buyers, have an ever-increasing ability to see where the '*what you really need*' message is a put-up job to shout your brand's benefits to your own best advantage. The critical test of any such positioning is that the factors chosen are of genuine importance to the customer. If they don't care about price then bragging about your supreme value for money is of little help – indeed, more likely to be a turn-off.

3. The value context

Step 2 will have helped us to identify the specific benefits that the brand must provide and communicate. Step 3 will put those benefits into a context of value – what are you getting for what you are giving? Here are the main options:

- **Getting more for more** – the '*reassuringly expensive*' Stella Artois, or premium-priced Häagen-Dazs or Starbucks.
- **Getting more for the same** – the Lexus. '*Perhaps the first time in history that trading a $72,000 car for a $36,000 car could be considered trading up*', runs one of its ads.
- **Getting more for less** – the so-called *category killer* retail brands such as Toys 'R' Us and Wal*Mart, where their scale and buying power promises bigger ranges, greater choice and lower prices.
- **Getting the same for less** – Tesco with its high-profile '*rip-off Britain*' campaign to sell Levi jeans at non-rip-off prices.

▦ **Getting less for much less** – 'stripped down' brands such as EasyJet, the Formule 1 hotel chain, or Aldi. These examples show that the *giving* part of the equation is not always money – it might be the sacrifice of amenities, an acceptance of risk, or a 'managed level of discomfort'.

The options that do not appear here, 'getting the same for more' and especially 'getting less for more', are two value contexts taken up by fast-declining brands!

4. The total customer experience

A key purpose of brand positioning is to ensure that the right interactions take place with the right customers. The sum of these interactions makes up what we will call the *total customer experience*. The more impactful and satisfying the brand manager can

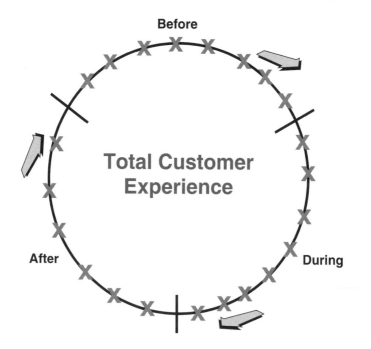

Figure 11.3 *The customer's activity cycle*

make this experience, the more valuable the brand. At this point we are moving into the territory of Part III, cementing the brand definition into the customer's mind. The brand manager should examine every possible interaction, mapping them out on what we might call the customer's activity cycle (see Figure 11.3).

The cycle starts with the realisation of a need, moves through the assessment of options, the decision to purchase, on to use, and then post-use satisfaction, disposal and the need to repurchase. Then ask the questions: 1) does the brand make a positive impact at every step? and 2) could it make more positive impacts, and where?

Virgin Atlantic

The Virgin Atlantic brand is particularly skilled at making positive impacts at points in the cycle as yet still unthought of by others. Take two examples.

We all hate those early-morning flights that demand check-ins at unearthly hours and so make us get up at even more unearthly hours of the night. Virgin Atlantic now offers the facility to check in the evening before, and then turn up for the flight at a more civilised hour – a positive impact on a previously unattended part of the activity cycle, and an addition to the brand's unique definition and positioning.

Or, imagine you are on holiday in Florida. You've had a great time with the family in the parks, until the last day, which is spent getting to the airport and hanging around with tearful and frustrated kids who just want to see Mickey one more time. So how about letting you check your luggage in at one of the parks, so that you can spend your last day on holiday rather than in transit? The Virgin Atlantic brand keeps itself ahead of the pack through such innovations, developed as a result of its understanding of and concern for the total customer experience. It has successfully created a brand that takes it well beyond the mundane business of just flying aircraft.

Now, post-11 September 2001, perhaps all this changes and these kind of interactions are either not possible or not desirable. Perhaps new interactions that stress and ensure security will become the mark of the leading airline brands – times change, but brands can react positively as well as defensively to these changes.

A vital choice – brands and expectations

Do you position the brand to meet existing customer expectations, or to change those expectations? History shows the former to have more chance of success, but the latter can be the path to spectacular riches if it succeeds, and the path to disaster if it fails. Brands that have tried to change the rules and failed are rarely remembered – the Sinclair C5 is an exception simply because of its unusually high profile audacity and its incredible ineptitude.

Some brands genuinely change the market – Microsoft, Sony Walkman, Wal*Mart and Amazon.com are well-known examples and there are many more less well known. They change the market because they have the audacity to meet needs that have not yet been expressed. Identifying these 'latent needs' is a skill and a science and an art wrapped into one.

Success depends ultimately on the strength of your proposition. The Sinclair C5's proposition was inherently weak; the Sony Walkman's was very powerful, if undreamt of by most of its future customers. The key to reducing the awesome risks in such a pursuit is market research and market testing, and the humility to listen to feedback and learn. We are back to our model of the learning brand introduced at the start of Part I.

Repositioning

Brands die (if you let them)

The 1950s was a boom period for concentrated fruit squash drinks, and Treetops was a leading brand with an eye-catching bottle design that still served it well into the design-conscious 1960s. The brand definition was about economy and thrift, and very appropriate for the time.

Today most of us will happily pay more for a 250ml bottle of flavoured mineral water than for a litre of squash that might make 20 pints. We will even pay a huge premium to have that same squash (though not Treetops) in a small cardboard box, ready diluted. The values of social expression and convenience have grown more significant in this market; some brands managed the transition, while some did not.

In some ways those brands with the strongest and most recognisable positioning have the hardest task of changing to move with the times. It is a feature of anachronisms that they were once absolutely spot on...

Some brands become liabilities and should be killed, or sold. Others may still provide a nice income stream as they are progressively run to grass. Then there are those brands with enough long-term value to make it worth the risk of repositioning. The risk is twofold – if you fail then not only is the investment lost, but now try going back to where you came from. The truth of the matter is that repositioning is probably harder than the initial positioning – there is the question of existing perceptions and beliefs. Rather than providing a good foundation on which to build, the existing brand heritage is often an obstacle to change.

Leaving home

It's the same with people. Imagine that someone wants to change their personality. They might change their clothes, their hairstyle, their accent, their behaviour, but the problem is that their family and friends still remember who they were before all this confusing messing about. If a person really wants to change their personality then the answer is usually to leave home. Repositioning a brand often involves much the same process.

Lucozade

Time was when Lucozade was what your mother bought for you when you were ill. Generations have grown up identifying the brand with illness and recuperation. It was a clear positioning but once it was well established the potential for growth was rather limited. SmithKline Beecham, the brand's owner, conducted a brilliant campaign over a number of years to reposition the product as a high-energy 'sports drink'. SB had identified the potential in this segment and it had a product with many of the necessary attributes. High-profile product endorsements from the likes of Daley Thompson were used to great effect alongside new packaging designs and new target retail outlets. Lucozade is still a favourite choice for those overcoming illness, but it now also occupies a position well away from the invalid's bedside table. The brand managed to select the appropriate parts of its existing definition and personality to act as a protective halo on its journey to its new home.

Changing the mood

Not all repositioning has to be this dramatic. Leaving home is an extreme step with extreme risks. Sometimes repositioning can be effected through changes of mood.

Predictor

Predictor, a self-use pregnancy testing kit, found that its personality was not entirely suited to its growth aspirations. The product was well thought of, reliable and responsible, but it suffered from some negative associated images – unpleasant surprises, let-downs, unwanted pregnancies. It was too often a product that you bought when trouble was looming. While that might have been a base on which to position the brand – a promise of performance in use – it wasn't where Predictor wanted to be. It wanted the brand to have a more upbeat emotional charge, and so a more prominent place in the customer's mind: personal fulfilment. A combination of a packaging redesign and an advertising campaign demonstrating the joy, private and public, of discovering your dreams come true helped to put the brand on to this new level.

Irn-Bru

Irn-Bru, a brand of fizzy drink with an almost fanatical following in Scotland, had for many years made much of its rather minimal iron content – *'made in Scotland from girders'*. It appealed to an increasingly ageing audience. Figure 11.4 illustrates the extraordinary change of mood developed, with great success, in order to build sales among the new generation of 'fizzy drinkers'.

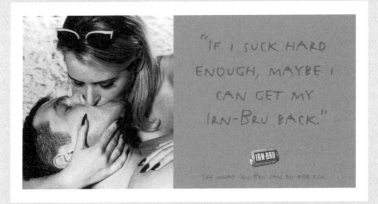

Figure 11.4 *Changing the mood*

The Irn-Bru case again illustrates the high-risk tendency of some brands to appeal to 'the in crowd' and in so doing risk the disapproval of those beyond the target audience – good segmentation is vital for such a strategy.

Changing with the times

Repositioning along with the changing times is the lowest-risk strategy, but calls for a surprising flexibility of mind. Its main obstacle is all those who cry out *'if it ain't broke, don't fix it'*, the death knell of many a brand.

Repositioning from behind

When a company is aware of a poor image for its product it will need to do more than just tell people how great it is. Humour is a favourite tack and there have been many adverts that appear to knock the advertiser as a means of changing people's perceptions. A TV ad for a Skoda car has a car park attendant apologising to a worried car owner (a Skoda owner) for the vandalism done to his car – some little devil has stuck a Skoda badge on the front. Humour, recognition of the current perceptions, and a clever point about how things have changed, yet some (not you, of course) are still behind the times.

12

Brand extension – *beyond wrinkle cream*

The product life cycle

Products and brands are like living things: they are born, they grow, they mature, and if nothing is done to prevent it, they grow old, decline and die. Figure 12.1 illustrates a typical product life cycle (PLC), but the brand manager should not be resigned to the inevitable fate that it suggests.

That a brand reaches maturity is often the result of its own success breeding a series of '*me too*' products that flood the market, spoiling the game for everyone. Of course, being first in has some advantages when it comes to customer awareness and loyalty, and if the brand can continue to distinguish itself from its '*Johnny-come-lately*' imitators then it can fend off the effects of maturity for longer.

Using the brand as a kind of anti-ageing cream can be effective, for a while, but in time the ageing process proves too much to resist. At this point, the brand's owners start to withdraw investment and the writing is on the wall.

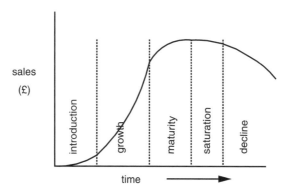

Figure 12.1 *The product life cycle*

Brand augmentation

Brand managers should be looking much further ahead than this. Even while the brand is growing, they should be laying plans for how they will give it a new lease of life. New packaging, new advertisements, new promotions, new associations – these are just some of the things that can be done to *augment* the brand. Designed to give the brand a 'kick', to set it on a new growth path away from the threat of maturity, the classic scenario is the '*new improved formulation*', whether it be soap powder or a motor car.

Cars are managed through this process to an increasingly preordained plan. The launch model is quite basic – its novelty being enough to ensure success. As time goes by, a stream of extras are applied; things once optional become standard. A sure sign of a car approaching the end of its life cycle is when it carries every conceivable extra as the standard offer.

In the grand scheme of things, brand augmentation is a relatively low-cost activity with attractive returns, but it can only be carried on for so long. Time comes when more radical changes are required.

Brand extension

Perhaps the time comes when maturity is inevitable whatever new augmentations are attempted. The brand managers still want to extract the most value from their assets but cannot see much more to be had in the existing market. Here their minds may turn to brand extension.

As many as two out of three new product launches are examples of brand extension. This is where an existing brand is used to support the launch of a new product. The reasons are clear – new product launches are very risky, most fail, and using the 'halo' of an existing brand (see Chapter 9) can help to reduce that risk. If the market is also new, then the risk is even greater and the halo effect yet more important. The problem is that if a brand extension fails, the backlash will be felt by the original brand.

Brand extension comes in different forms. The simplest is the launch of the existing product in a new format. Soap powder takes on a liquid form under the same brand name, or Mars Bars are shrunk into bite-size pieces and launched as Mars Little Ones. Some would argue that this was really still brand augmentation, with the brand chasing much the same market with much the same product – or does the Mars Little Ones proposition target a new buyer in a new circumstance? This is more than playing with words – augmentation is relatively safe territory, dealing with what you know already; genuine extension enters the higher risk zone.

Next up the ladder of extension is the launch of what we might call companion products under the same name. Gillette razor blades will add Gillette razors, and then Gillette shaving foam. Once each brand extension is successfully established, the process of brand augmentation will recommence, adding Gillette shaving gel to the shaving foam range, and so on.

The highest-risk brand extension is when the brand leaves its own territory. Virgin, as we have seen, is adept at this, reducing the risk through use of the brand halo effect, and ensuring that it translates the existing brand values to the new market.

Caterpillar has had success with its rugged outdoor clothing line, as has JCB, which has also moved into children's toys – with mini yellow diggers in abundance. These are extensions that 'make sense', which is to say that the target customer can see the relevance and accept the translated brand values. For JCB, durability, functionality and a rugged outdoor quality were all values and images that could be transferred to a range of clothing. Some extensions make less sense.

Cosmopolitan took its brand into yoghurts and flavoured mineral waters, Philip Morris considers taking the Marlboro brand into hotels. Some brand extensions come naturally; some are forced for reasons of growth targets – dangerous ground for the brand manager.

Looking ahead to an idea to be discussed further in Chapter 14, we might think of the brand's definition as its DNA, its unique signature. Brand extension, or 'brand stretching' as it is sometimes called, stretches the DNA. Do we reach a point where one stretch too many weakens the genes and we start breeding half-wits and chinless wonders?

Brand architecture – putting it all together

Almost anything can be branded: products, services, people, places, even ideas. If everything can be branded, and most companies have more than one product or activity, how are we to avoid an overwhelming and ultimately damaging cacophony of brands just within the same business, let alone the same market? There is a need for some order and method, and this is where *brand architecture* comes in.

Brands are used in an amazing variety of configurations. KitKat is a brand, but so too is Nestlé, its owner, and so we have Nestlé KitKat. Does that combination of brand names strengthen or diminish KitKat as a brand? Nestlé clearly believes the former, but what of Nestlé Sarsons or Nestlé Crosse & Blackwell – two brands put up for sale by the food giant in 2002?

Unilever has over 1,500 different brands in use around the world, most of which we would not identify with the parent company, while almost everything that Microsoft, Virgin, Mitsubishi, Yamaha or Shell do – and it's a great variety – goes under the same *corporate* name.

The need for a variety of architectures

Brand architecture is the study of these different configurations, but before we describe some of the principal 'designs' we should ask why there is a need for these different approaches. Such an understanding will help us to avoid the jerry-built results of poor architectural design. Brands can be strengthened or weakened as a result of their place in the grand design.

Let's take as our starting point a company with a number of existing brands and some potential new ones in the pipeline. They face the question: should these brands be developed as independent entities, or might they benefit from being built into a more uniform architecture?

The matrix shown in Figure 13.1 (developed from a concept introduced by Professor Peter Doyle to consider the desirability of building corporate brands) will help us to answer this question. The vertical axis asks whether the various markets targeted by these brands are broadly similar to each other or display significant differences. The key to sameness or difference is usually to be found in the behaviours and attitudes of the target customers. The horizontal axis asks whether the values expressed by each brand proposition (the brand definition) and expected by the customer are broadly similar to each other or whether they display significant differences.

The more alike the different markets that are targeted, and the more similar the brand values, then the more scope there is for a *corporate brand* with all its benefits of efficiency and economies of scale. Where there is no similarity between markets and the brand values are quite distinct for each proposition, then the greater the need for unique *product brands*. There are two other options shown in this matrix, to be discussed in full below: what we will call the *validated identity brand*, and the *sub-brand* or *mark*.

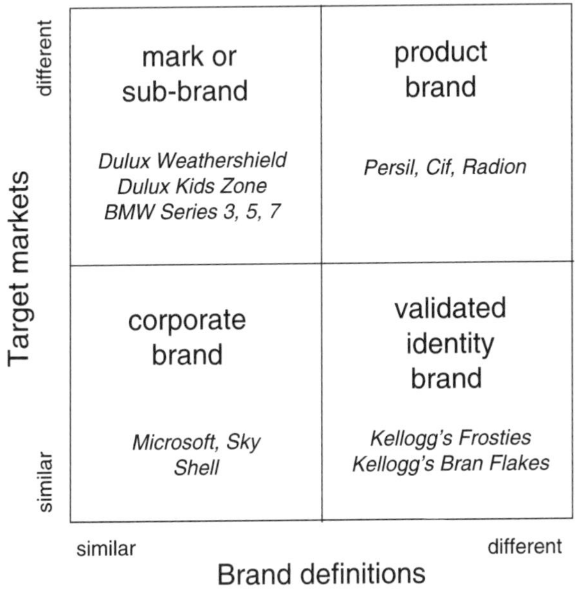

	different	mark or sub-brand *Dulux Weathershield Dulux Kids Zone BMW Series 3, 5, 7*	product brand *Persil, Cif, Radion*
Target markets		corporate brand *Microsoft, Sky Shell*	validated identity brand *Kellogg's Frosties Kellogg's Bran Flakes*
	similar	similar	different
		Brand definitions	

Figure 13.1 *Brand architecture*
With acknowledgements to Professor Peter Doyle

And why does this matter? Think of the brand as a personality. Would you expect one individual to be equally convincing in front of audiences with widely differing expectations? Can the same comedian, with the same act, get the same laughs from a working men's club in Wigan and a vicarage garden party in Esher? You wouldn't think of booking the same turn for both occasions, so why do we sometimes expect as much from our brands? How would you feel about receiving as a gift a nice box of Boeing chocolates? Not *too* bad? So how about flying to Australia on a Cadbury 747?

Sometimes imposing a corporate brand or a validated identity brand could seriously limit the potential of a product brand, or a new product launch.

Ford, Toyota and Honda

Ford struggled for years to move into the higher-priced luxury end of the car market and in the end found it easier to buy Jaguar in order to achieve its ends. Rebadging the Jaguar as a Ford would have been a disaster. The high emotional charge of car brands makes it a particularly interesting case in this debate. Toyota chose to launch its new quality car under the Lexus brand, Honda chose to create the Acura brand, because the target markets were sufficiently different from its current ones and its planned brand definitions were also very different.

Product brands

Let's start with the simplest architecture – a product brand. We have three unique and independent products, and each has a unique and independent brand name – Persil, Cif, Radion. A company may operate several brands; these are just three of Unilever's 1,500 plus world-wide, but it still regards and manages each one as a separate entity with its own unique name. The reason behind such apparent inefficiency is simple – each brand targets a unique customer group, and each brand has a unique definition. This is so fundamental to the strength of a brand, its evidencing of a unique match between capabilities and customer needs, that any pursuer of business efficiency through brand consolidation should be very cautious before they act to destroy value built over many years.

Whitbread

A few years back, if you took a walk around a large market town you might find as many as eight restaurants owned by the same parent, Whitbread. The restaurants went under different product brands – Pizza Hut, Pizzaland, Dome, TGI Friday's, Costa Coffee, Jim Thompson's Spice Island Trading, Beefeater,

Brewer's Fayre – and most of their clientele would not have known the link. Why should they? What advantage would Whitbread have gained from that? The people in each restaurant were quite different, a credit to Whitbread's ability to link segmentation with branding. There would only be room for one Whitbread-branded restaurant in the town (and it would then probably be mistaken for a pub by those of us over 30).

Sub-brands and marks

Where a supplier has different products placed in different and distinct markets, but wishes to share some common values across them, or to transfer the values from an existing product to a new one, then the use of a sub-brand architecture can work well. This is quite typical in the car market, where the essential values that define the brand are appreciated by all its customers, but some have larger budgets (or aspirations) than others, hence the BMW 3 series, 5 series and 7 series – different *marks* of the same brand.

Validated identity brands

Some product brands choose to make more of their parent company's name – Kellogg's Frosties, Kellogg's Bran Flakes, Kellogg's Rice Krispies and so on. Different from pure product brands, these are sometimes called *family* brands, *umbrella* brands or *validated identity* brands, and this last name suggests the purpose. Individual product brands can be given greater authority by making it clear whose stable they come from. Kellogg's provides a protective umbrella to product brands that might not stand up so well on their own – would Pop Tarts have been launched as successfully without such a validated identity? And how about cornflakes? Such a common name or simple descriptor of a product is hard to register as a brand in the legal sense, but by putting it under a validated identity 'umbrella', Kellogg's Corn Flakes becomes a brand that stands out from its paler imitators.

An important point here is that the validated identity approach can work well when all of the products under the umbrella are in the same or similar markets – in this case breakfast cereals. But what if we go beyond that? How would we feel about Kellogg's bathroom scourer? It can be done, of course, but we are moving into a different kind of brand architecture here, to be discussed below – *corporate* branding.

When does a product brand become a validated identity brand? The dividing line is not clear, but it might be said that if the company name is bigger or better known, or carries more value than the product brand name, then that's a validated identity brand. Persil is not such a brand. Lever's name may appear on the box, but it is not Lever's Persil, it's just Persil. The question for the brand manager is – will attaching the company name enhance or reduce the brand?

Nestlé

When Nestlé purchased Rowntrees and in so doing acquired the KitKat brand, it quickly put its own name in place of Rowntrees'. Many accused it of throwing away value built over decades, but Nestlé simply believed that KitKat had sufficient value that was separate from its old parent, and that Nestlé provided just as good a validation as Rowntrees, as well as offering savings through uniformity and efficiency. Many might still beg to differ.

Corporate brands

One of the most contentious issues in branding over recent years has been the value, or otherwise, of the corporate brand. There are four broad arguments:

1. That this is simply an exercise in corporate egotism that has little value for the brand or for the customer.
2. That huge cost savings can be had through corporate branding (but beware of handing the management of your brands over to the accountants).
3. That this is a matter of culture, and some believe that culture can be changed.
4. That some very positive synergies are to be had when uniform corporate values can be applied across a range of different products, businesses and markets.

It's just a Japanese thing...

Turning to culture, we can see that the Japanese have long accepted the benefits of corporate brands. You can buy a Yamaha-branded motorbike, hi-fi, piano, yacht or electronic organ, without being unduly confused. This is not just a Japanese phenomenon. In India the Tata brand encompasses almost every business activity from banking to motor cars and FMCG to industrial chemicals. Such brands break the architectural 'rules' shown in Figure 13.1, but they succeed for reasons well understood in Japan, and slowly being realised elsewhere.

Back in Japan, Mitsubishi uses as one of its corporate slogans, '*From noodles to atomic power*', a statement that calls on a very Japanese perception of the role and status of business in society. Would the British be as happy trusting atomic power to Heinz, makers of spaghetti hoops?

A much-quoted study carried out by the Henley Centre in the 1990s showed that in the United Kingdom many consumer brands are trusted more than the police or the royal family. This and other similar studies also showed that we trust consumer brands more than their corporate owners. Among those brands winning high levels of trust were Pepsi, Mars and St Michael (product brands), while among the less trusted were Shell, Microsoft and Sky (corporate brands).

It would seem that, in the United Kingdom at least, a product brand, particularly one with a clear personality and compelling emotional charge, can be loved and cherished, while we remain wary of big business. Of course, it depends on the particular big business as to whether a corporate brand is good or bad for sales.

Shell's tussles with environmental groups on issues to do with exploration and drilling can have an impact on how we see its products at the pump. Sky's arguments with the Manchester United supporters' club can have an impact on its image quite out of proportion to the scale of the particular dispute. Companies that appear to the media, or to the government, to be growing too powerful, such as Microsoft, can have consequent problems with their brand image in the eyes of the consumer.

But if the big business in question establishes a 'good' reputation then it can of course transfer that to a good brand image. What we are saying here is that a big business can become a brand, and express certain values through that brand. Virgin is a case in point, with values that express a championing of the customer, breaking with convention, and sounding a challenge to existing norms and authorities.

The lesson taught by those that succeed in the pursuit of a corporate brand is that such a brand can sometimes play on a higher level of awareness and impact than the product brand. A product brand must identify and match the needs, attitudes and aspirations of a targeted market segment – it is necessarily concerned with the small picture. The corporate brand's definition requires a big picture approach, building values that match the political, social and economic mood of the time. So long as big business is venerated in Japan, corporate brands such as Mitsubishi and Yamaha will thrive, but economic failure, the end of the 'job for life' culture, and a few too many corporate scandals could lead to a rethink.

Virgin as an attribute brand

Sir Richard Branson calls Virgin an *'attribute brand'*, arguing that it has a value of its own quite independent from the specific product to which it might be attached. The brand is a reputation, and in this regard Virgin follows the Japanese practice. Branson has indeed attacked what he calls the *'stilted Anglo-Saxon view of consumers'* that insists a brand must relate directly to a product. Much of Virgin's success as a corporate brand has been to do with its ability to portray the Virgin business as a role model of good and modern business practice.

Positive synergies: the real purpose...

There are generally two types of synergies to be had from corporate branding: economic synergies and brand value synergies. That economies of scale and certain efficiencies of operation can be had from a corporate brand when working in diverse markets should never make this the prime mover for corporate branding. These are benefits that result from the architecture, but the reason the architecture works (if it does) is to be found in the corporate brand's ability to transfer uniform and consistent brand values across those different markets.

Virgin

Virgin's corporate brand values are around challenging the status quo as the consumer's champion. It loves to take on the 'establishment' in whatever market it places itself, and this value is personified in Sir Richard Branson, entrepreneur, adventurer, and friend of the consumer. There is always a new twist to any Virgin venture, a twist that makes use of those corporate values. It didn't just sell PEPs (personal equity plans), it took out the middleman. It doesn't just fly aircraft, it gets you to the airport on a Harley-Davidson limo-bike (and there's no reason why brands shouldn't borrow from others to help build their own definition).

Hotels with 'standby' tariffs, mobile phones with attitude, and bridal shops for brides (not just the bride's mother), these are all applications of the corporate brand values – championing the customer in style. The success of the Virgin corporate brand depends on the continuing relevance of those values. It is notable that Sir Richard Branson has made it clear that he wishes Virgin to be the most respected brand, not necessarily the biggest, and in corporate branding reputation is all.

Now comes a choice. Should the business seek to build a corporate brand definition that is of a sufficiently high level to be applied to almost any market circumstances, or does it only operate in markets where the corporate brand definition will make sense? Could Boeing chocolates and the Cadbury's 747 be made to work? Yes of course, given time, much effort, and a radical rethink of the essential brand values involved – but there might still be little point... with branding, synergies are not perhaps always a goal worth the chase.

Some downsides of the corporate brand

'*If it don't fit, don't force it*' is good advice in this matter. There are other risks. Does putting all your eggs in one basket over-stretch the credibility of that basket? Sir Richard Branson for one thinks that it doesn't have to:

> *Each time Virgin entered a new business all the conventional pundits whined that we were stretching our brand too far. Rather than worrying too much about brands being stretched too far, people will have to stretch their imaginations further.*

Of course, the imagination is a powerful thing, and how might it work if when you are sitting stranded somewhere between London and Manchester, *on a Virgin train*, and your mind turns to that flight you have booked to Johannesburg, next week, *on a Virgin plane...*

If a company like Nestlé *were* to have all its products under the one name, what would be the impact on the supermarket shelf? It could end up looking rather like one of those 'despised' private labels... Or if it was hit by a food scare on one of its products, how might that impact on all its other products?

Global or local brands?

Another choice to be made with your brand architecture is the decision to be global or local. Theodore Levitt set the scene for the global brand back in 1983 when he asserted that '*The world's needs and desires have been irrevocably homogenised.*' It was doubtful that they had in all but a few markets, but this became the mantra of brand managers seeking a global pitch.

The eighteenth 'immutable law' of branding, according to Al Ries, is that all brands should be global brands, and he cites Heineken as an example of a brand that knows no borders. Good example, and *if you can do it* then the benefits are enormous, but where does that leave segmentation and positioning? In very few markets do we find that '*the world*' is a useful segment. Would you sell vodka in France in the same way you would sell it in Poland? In truth, Heineken do not make that attempt – the brand name may be global, but the brand definition has some very local treatments.

ICI

In 1999, ICI Paints sold its Autocolor brand to long-time rival PPG. Autocolor was the paint brand for the car refinish market, the '*you bend 'em, we mend 'em*' business, as insiders called it. Some observers were surprised: the business was a success and a technical jewel in the ICI crown, but as a global brand it was a non-starter. John McAdam, executive VP for coatings at ICI, was clear about the sale: '*Technical markets are global... if you are not in the top three – forget it.*'

Things are different in the decorative paint market. Back in the 1980s when ICI bought in quick succession a number of leading brand names around the world – including Valentine in France and Glidden in the United States – the plan was set for a process of *'Duluxization'* – the creation of a truly global brand. No more; as John McAdam points out, *'Decorative markets are different from technical ones because you can be No 1 in the United Kingdom and be nowhere in Italy.'* Instead, the policy is to use local brands where they have strengths and resonances and to build a global portfolio of strong brands that includes Dulux, Glidden, Valentine, Cuprinol, Hammerite, Polyfilla and Polycell. John McAdam concedes, *'We thought we could apply a UK solution to the United States, without doing regional research.'*

Making global brands work

We find some of the same elements as in the debate over corporate or product brands; the economies of scale that global brands can bring (though never forget the staggering costs of their upkeep) versus the need to recognise local differences. Global brands can stand local variation, of course – Kentucky Fried Chicken is essentially the same brand in Japan as in the United States, but without the coleslaw – the Japanese don't go for coleslaw, and the KFC management call that a no-brainer. Global brands with local customisation can turn over time into quite distinct brands, without assiduous management. It is a difficult line for the brand manager to follow – they must be ever vigilant for variations that might actually change the brand's personality and values, while not becoming seen as the 'Gestapo' of the business. Remember that brands must evolve and that a 'thought police' approach can only bring stagnation.

Care is required at both ends of the spectrum. Perhaps the greatest care should be taken to avoid corporate egos getting into the brand's driving seat. Brands, global or otherwise, may be managed by the boardroom, but they should be driven by the market. National and cultural differences are still huge despite the ever-shrinking world, and there is still positive advantage in tailoring a brand to find a unique match with a local need. It's called finding a competitive edge.

We have come through many manifestations of how to deal with the apparently shrinking world. First came the rather brutal 'one size fits all' approach, particularly from the United States, with all the concomitant charges of US imperialism. Then we had the softening *'think global, act local'* approach. *Glocal*, with its underlying desire to demonstrate that *'we're all the same really...* ', brought some uncomfortable stereotyping, and then came the rather ephemeral idea that we are one 'global village' – less a statement of the brotherhood of man and more a clumsy attempt to find workable global segments. Now it would seem that we are back to *'think local, act local'* – at least, that is the view of Douglas Daft, CEO of Coca-Cola, the world's most truly global brand.

Daft quite rightly dismisses the idea of there being a market segment called 'the world': '*We were looking at similarities, not differences, and we didn't stand for anything in particular for the individual.*'

It will be interesting to see just how far Coca-Cola allows the development of local brand definitions to go and how keen the local management is to take up its new freedoms.

Part III

Brand management – the implementation

While brand positioning was about finding or creating a relevant space in the customer's mind, implementing the brand is about cementing the brand definition into that space. At this point, we could easily expand to five more books of this size with guidance on the naming, packaging and advertising of your brand, not to mention the building of positive associations and the development of additional interactions with customers. Limited space is, however, a virtue on this occasion. Most of these activities are jobs for the experts. What seemed a great name 'down the pub' can fast lose its magic when seen emblazoned on the product (witness those truly cringeworthy company names painted on the back doors of countless vans driven by plumbers, electricians, builders *et al* – how about 'Ubends "R" us'?). Likewise, advertising is an expensive game, and enthusiastic amateurs can make some very costly mistakes. Advertisements written by brand managers or, worse, the CEO can be spotted a mile away.

This is not a book for professional copywriters, packaging designers or other media experts. It is a guide for those who own and manage brands and who need to know what all those experts will be getting up to on their behalf. Only then will they be able to manage them effectively. This, then, is the approach taken in Part III, everything you need to know, but not so much that you might consider doing it yourself!

Building positive associations – the moments of truth

It is the brand manager's responsibility to ensure that every brand interaction with the customer builds and enhances the brand's definition. This includes the choice of the name, the logo, the packaging design, the sales approach, the management of customer relationships, the advertising, the appearance at the point of sale, the characteristics of the product or service in use, after-sales support and, not to be forgotten, the handling of complaints. Each one of these 'steps along the way' is an opportunity for a positive customer interaction, and each one is what we might call a *moment of truth* for the brand.

Chapter 15 will focus on advertising's moments of truth, while here we will focus on some of the ingredients that can help build positive associations and cement the brand's definition into the customer's mind:

- the name;
- logos and slogans;
- packaging;
- customer relationships;
- inventing new interactions and associations.

What's in a name?

A new brand can have a name specially designed to suit its definition; an old brand is stuck with what it has inherited. How much does this matter, and should a brand ever consider changing its name? Plenty of product brands carry their founder's or inventor's name, though we have long since stopped making associations with any real person, and are often surprised that there was indeed a Mr Firestone or a Mr Goodyear.

Almost any name can grow to represent the brand definition, *provided it has time*. Of course, a good word with positive associations can also become associated with a poor brand definition – Lada is Russian for 'beloved'.

'*What's in a name? That which we call a rose / By any other name would smell as sweet.*' Al Ries argues that Shakespeare, at least when it comes to brand names, was wrong, '*which is why the single most important decision in the marketing of perfume is the name*'.

Choosing a word or name that sounds like or might even be confused with another attention-grabbing word is another approach – 'fcuk' being perhaps the most controversial of recent times – it's just an abbreviation, they say, for French Connection UK.

Acronyms and abbreviations can of course become brand names, and it is often a surprise when we learn their original meaning. 3M says innovation and invention, hardly words that the Minnesota Mining and Manufacturing Company would bring to mind. Who would be enthused by the products of the Bayerische Motoren Werke? BMW to you and me.

Certain letters appear more commonly in brand names than in normal everyday use, the letters x, k and o being the most notable. Dulux, Kodak, Knorr, IKEA, Exxon, Xerox and Oxo are just some of many that attract our attention through their unusual appearance. Kodak was coined by George Eastman in 1888, being '*short, vigorous, incapable of being misspelled... and in order to satisfy trademark laws it must mean nothing*'. Not a bad formula. We might extend Eastman's formula a little, to say that a brand name should meet at least the majority of the following criteria:

- **Short and vigorous.** They don't come much shorter or more vigorous than Oxo, or the new football boot brand from Umbro – Xai.
- **Incapable of being misspelt or mispronounced.** Though Knorr and Nestlé have successfully ignored this criterion for decades.
- **Unique to the brand.** The search for a unique name can be long and frustrating – it's amazing what has already been dreamt up...
- **Consistent with the desired brand definition.** Old names will have already grown into this position, new ones must be chosen with care – Häagen-Dazs is a pure invention, but has all the right Scandinavian connotations to be intriguing and suggests some expertise in things icy...
- **Must sit within the existing brand architecture.** 'Sane' might be a great name for a new hotel chain that specialises in stress-reducing therapeutic stays, but perhaps not so good if it is included as a sub-brand under the Holiday Inn umbrella...
- **Capable of international usage without causing embarrassment or cultural offence.** Ignored successfully by the likes of fcuk, and ignored to its cost by Chrysler when launching the Nova motor car in Mexico ('no va' means 'doesn't go').
- **Capable of grabbing attention.** fcuk certainly keeps this rule at least.
- **Capable of being protected.** Not a common word or simple descriptor: a word that means nothing will fit the bill nicely, but might end up meaning just that – nothing.
- **Liked by the target audience...** Research and more research... and don't rely on one drunken session of the marketing team.

Here is some provocative advice from Lexicon, a brand development company:

1. 'Are we comfortable with the name? Then it's OK but not great' – a great brand name should provoke.
2. 'Does the name break any rules? If not, try again' – a great brand name needs to do better than just fit in.
3. 'Can we use the name to make a promise or tell a story?' – this is a 'must have'.

Is 'owning the word' good for a brand?

Some regard it as a strength of a brand name that it becomes the generic for a product or service – to *Hoover* the carpet, to *Sellotape* a package, and then to *FedEx* it to Sydney. But how often have you hoovered the carpet with a Dyson, sellotaped with Scotch Tape, or FedEx-ed that package by DHL? How often have you ordered a Coke in a café and been served an anonymous cola without comment?

Awareness through use of your brand name as the generic is a great thing, but we have seen that branding is about more than simple awareness; it is about associations. If customers will happily associate other people's products with your brand name, then where does this leave your own brand definition?

Becoming the generic is good, provided that you really *do* own the word, and continue to retain that ownership. That takes massive and continuous investment, continued vigilance, continuing evolution, and a refusal to rest on your laurels. A great and glorious heritage is not enough.

There are other ways of *owning the word*. Lotus owns *spreadsheet*, Iomega owns *stuff*, and perhaps FedEx owns *overnight*. Good positive associations all.

Changing the name

Great outrage, letters to *The Times* and much free publicity attend the change of a well-known brand name. Remember when Marathon became Snickers and Opal Fruits became Starbursts? It was as though a part of your childhood was being stolen.

The cost can be huge – when Andersen Consulting was forced to change to Accenture, the total bill was reputed to be well over £100 million – so why do it if not forced? The pursuit of global consistency is the reason behind Snickers and Starbursts and, managed well, the change can cause less disruption to sales or loyalty than the letters of outrage might have suggested.

Timing can be everything in such matters. Unilever resisted for years switching the name Jif, used in the United Kingdom, to Cif, the name used across all of continental Europe. Cif was thought to sound too much like the slang for a particular type of venereal disease. The rise of Aids has taken the attention off such 'second-grade ailments' and Cif is now thought thoroughly safe and respectable.

Other reasons can involve needing to change a name that has just grown out of date, or is too restrictive in its scope. The Post Office became Consignia, a name that it believed reflects its international standing. The change might have confused and even upset many of its UK-based customers, but overseas it can be seen why 'the Post Office' is not the most helpful of names. The name change did not last, and the company is now called Royal Mail Group plc.

Perhaps in the end it is just a way to give a flagging brand a new lease of life through all the attention the change brings – '*the artist formerly known as Prince*' comes to mind.

Logos and slogans

Logos

Figure 14.1 is perhaps all that needs to be said about the importance of a good and consistently used logo.

The logo is the fast means to recognition, eliciting subconscious responses that can often tip the balance of the sale. B2B

Figure 14.1 *The importance of the logo*

brands should never underestimate the power of a logo in this regard – for many years, the best-selling fertiliser in the agricultural market was ICI's 'blue bag'. The ICI roundel and the familiar blue bag were all the farmer needed to see to convince him of the product's quality – the logo represented the firm's reputation and became one of the most familiar sites in barns across the United Kingdom. And of course, once your logo is recognised, resist the temptation to change it every year.

Slogans

Slogans can be dangerous things; they have a habit of backfiring when times change. British Rail's '*This is the age of the train*' was coined on a wave of enthusiasm for public transport that soon dissolved, and the slogan looked less and less convincing with every passing year. '*Let's make things better*', a slogan from Philips, the Dutch electronics firm, was a sitting duck for any headline writer each time the company had a product flop or a serious customer complaint.

In trying to expand customer perceptions beyond the obvious, the Post Office adopted the slogan '*Delivering value*', but too many found it an easy potshot, saying that they would prefer it if the Post Office just managed to deliver letters.

Sometimes slogans can be too clever. '*Guinnless isn't good for you*' back in 1984 perhaps called for too many second takes. Think of slogans as short-term tactics, not fundamentals of the brand definition.

Packaging – the Cinderella of branding

The packaging industry has been under much pressure in recent years, with buyers more interested in reducing costs than in adding value. The tragedy of this is that packaging, used well, provides huge scope for building brand definition through customer interaction.

KitKat

Even KitKat has succumbed to the cost and efficiency argument in preference to enhancing the brand's interactions with its customers. The new flow-wrap packaging certainly reduces costs, but dropping the tin foil wrapper means the loss of a significant part of the consumer experience. A small but important interaction with the consumer has been removed, and what is still a therapeutic break-time treat has edged just a little closer to being a chocolate wafer biscuit.

Packaging exists for many reasons: to ship, to protect, to preserve, to identify, to help in use, to store and to dispose. We should also add to this list, to help build the brand:

- Consider a paint brand with a brand definition of 'colour and transformation'. Wouldn't it be great if the paint cans were transparent so that customers could see the real colour and not just a tiny colour chip?
- Limmits, the range of slimming biscuits, come in slim shapes with silky black wrappers, *'just as I would like to be'*, say many of its consumers, *'slim and sexy'*.
- Consider a fine malt whisky that has built a brand definition through images of peat bogs and faithful retainers. It has worked hard to distinguish itself from those ordinary blended whiskies, and yet there it sits on the off-licence shelf, just another bottle of brown spirit. Enter the cardboard tube

– a small step for packaging, but a giant leap for the sales of high-quality whisky, particularly if purchased as a gift…

▨ Consider a brand of photographic film that centres its brand definition on perfect colour representation. How will it look if the boxes lined up on the shelf vary in hue from dark to light?

▨ The Angostura Bitters bottle positively screams its unique individuality – the label is way too large, the text on it far too small, but it is instantly recognisable and it works.

▨ The toilet duck was a brilliant example of a brand capturing a unique identity, both visually through the distinctive shape of the bottle, but also emotionally through our belief that now we really can reach those germs that have been stubbornly evading us.

▨ If your business is in the supply of bulk materials to industrial customers, how could new packaging help identify your brand as the easiest to handle, to store, to maintain or to renew?

▨ Even in disposing of the product, the packaging can give the brand one last customer interaction. The Evian brand has made good use of plastic bottles that can be crushed down to a quarter of their original size after use. A brand that stresses the purity and ecological soundness of its product has successfully added another positive association to its image – the reduction of landfill on disposal.

Customer relationships

Managing the human moments of truth

Every human point of contact must also aim to build positive associations.

SAS

Jan Carlzon, when CEO of SAS, described these human points of contact as the brand's *'moments of truth'* and he went on to quantify them. SAS looked after 5 million passengers a year, and each passenger would probably meet five members of SAS staff. That meant that there would be 25 million SAS brand moments of truth, 25 million opportunities to build and enhance the brand, but also 25 million opportunities to let the brand down. Sales and customer service training became high priorities to support the SAS brand definition.

NCR

Back in the 19th century when NCR was just building up momentum for its new-fangled cash registers, a key element of the brand was the sales presentation. It was so important that a detailed guide on how to behave was issued to all sales representatives, including such gems as *'don't point your finger or pencil at the prospect, don't sit awkwardly in your chair, don't slap him on the knee, and don't tell funny stories'*. For a retail, service or B2B brand, the sales force can often make or break the brand's identity and definition.

The complaint is a gift...

Learning brands must learn from the complaints they receive. More than this, how those complaints are handled is of huge importance to the maintenance of the brand's definition.

TV watchdog programmes will go to great lengths to chastise a famous brand that has let the customer down. The brand manager who vacillates with weasel words is on a hiding to nothing. The brand manager who responds with bucketloads of apologies and enough free product to last the customer a lifetime gets away with it, but is the customer satisfied, and what of the millions of others watching at home, with no free products?

In too many cases the brand manager takes the easy route of a voucher or a free sample. I know of several big brands for which if you simply send them a letter saying that you bought the product *in one of the big retailers*, and you are not happy, you will get a bundle of vouchers by return.

Brand managers should ensure that they move into overdrive to investigate a problem. And when they discover the causes – report them to the customer, put right the problem, and give evidence of a better level of reliability in the future.

Inventing new interactions and associations

Borders and Barnes & Noble, two US booksellers, pioneered the invention of several new interactions with their customers – armchairs, in-store coffee shops, meeting spaces for societies, barber shop choirs... Who could name a bookstore brand before all that?

A good source of positive associations is to be found in other people's brands. Little Chef features Bird's custard on its menu, McDonald's builds its brand through the use of the likes of Cadbury's and Nestlé in its product lines, and of course the arrangement is mutual. Heineken has often associated itself with other brands' imagery – including a healed up cut in a piece of silk, and famously, the Dulux dog seen painting a wall – all part of the '*reaches the parts that other beers cannot reach*' campaign.

A brand can benefit by building on the stories that some-times attach themselves. Ford has not suffered from the '*any colour so long as it's black*' tale, Ben & Jerry is the subject of countless urban myths (in the United States at least) of what it does with its profits and what causes it supports, and The Body Shop benefited hugely from the high profile the media gave to its founder and campaigner for all sorts, Anita Roddick. A charismatic boss can be a great asset to a brand or a business – even the ICI 'brand' became 'exciting' under the leadership of John Harvey-Jones.

Cadbury World

Cadbury World is one of the few tourist attraction 'theme parks' run by a brand that is not primarily in the entertainment business. Many say it has no business to be doing this, not least some within the company, who could point out that it has lost money for more years than it has turned a profit. Of course, it is there for reasons other than profit – its financial target is in fact to break even. Cadbury World helps cement the brand's definition – quality and fun. It doesn't exploit the brand, it helps to build the brand, and the vast majority of its millions of visitors will have had their perception of the brand enhanced by this wonderfully creative and wholly positive interaction.

B2B brands can perhaps benefit the most from extending their customer interactions beyond the confines of their products. Selling services and solutions rather than products is a common strategy, but it is not always easy to get the due reward. Using a brand to identify the package of services and solutions as a distinct entity, separate from the competitor's 'product', can help enormously.

Finally, a brand can always use a little help from associations with liked and respected personalities, provided of course that they are the *right* people for the brand. You own a brand of jeans aimed at 'cool' teenagers; how pleased would you be if the Prime Minister took to wearing them? What goes for 'cool' is endlessly surprising and the oddest folk can become icons of teenage cool, so who knows...

The internet interaction...

Of course, the internet has provided a whole new medium for interaction with many consumer brands operating websites that offer product information, deals, and very often advice that helps position the brand on a much wider footing. The Pampers website has become a popular source of advice on all aspects of mothering, so taking the brand definition far beyond a simple supplier of nappies.

The interaction is two-way, providing information to the brand owners on how to steer their brand positioning in the future. The consumer is given a new channel of enquiry in this exchange, and with equal access to competitors' sites there is an increase in the transparency of the brand for the consumer. Choice is made easier, comparisons are made easier and, in some cases, genuine enquiry into value received can be made. In this way, the internet promises to keep brands on their toes as much as it gives them a new medium of interaction.

There is a dilemma here for the typical FMCG branded product. Consumers tend to buy baskets of groceries, not individual products, so won't the brand's website inevitably lose out to the retailers? The offer of advice through the website is one response, but perhaps there are more cunning ones in store. Where would you expect to find information on Jaffa Cakes? In the McVities site, or on a kids' site? Put yourself in the shoes of the consumer...

Swatch

Swatch is keen to make a radically new but hugely relevant association between its brand and the notion of time. Universal or internet time, 'launched' in 1998, divides the day into 1,000 beats, and time zones are gone. Should it catch on, who knows what we might be saying in years to come? 'Swatch Time' in place of Greenwich Mean, even 'log in with me at 8 o'Swatch'? – a powerful association indeed.

Advertising – not the whole story

It will be clear by now that branding is not just an exercise in advertising. If it becomes so, then it runs the risk of being seen as an expensive, untrustworthy and ultimately ephemeral activity. Advertising is important, but it is far from the whole story.

Having no budget for advertising does not mean that you cannot have a brand. There can be a virtue in small budgets; they demand hard thinking and subtlety, whereas huge budgets can lead to laziness and bludgeoning. Indeed, having a small budget can sometimes be worse than none at all. A few tens of thousands wasted on a tacky (and all too obviously home-made) advert can do more to harm a brand than almost any other activity short of making a bad product. This is particularly true of B2B brands.

If a brand is no more than its advertising, if it lacks substance in the final assessment, then it runs a big risk of being 'found out'. Sunny Delight was a big hit in the 1990s when Procter & Gamble launched this orange juice lookalike, but with almost no real juice. It certainly made lots of money for P&G but is now headed into decline as consumers start to 'get smart'. The kind of brand advertising that lasts is often the kind that has solid connections to the reality of the product – '*Have a break, have a KitKat*' celebrates both the break-time use and the 'snapability' of the thing.

Why advertise?

There is a difference between advertising and brand advertising. The former may be simply to get attention, to boost sales, to inform about an offer or any one of countless other goals. Brand advertising is intended to build and communicate the brand's definition. If both can be achieved at the same time then all well and good, but don't assume that simply mentioning your brand name a lot will build the image that you desire. The promotional philosophy that if you throw enough mud at the wall some of it is bound to stick has no place in the process of building your brand.

Advertising is part of the mix alongside the product, the service, the packaging, the point of sale and the price – and all of this must support the brand's positioning. There are many reasons that advertising tends to get an inflated level of attention, not least because we all think we are experts, and we all have an opinion. At its worst this leads to the horrors of the home-made ad. There are also some more justifiable reasons:

▦ It costs a lot of money.
▦ Done badly the whole proposition can collapse.
▦ Done well, advertising can represent that whole mix.

Brand advertising should concern itself with communicating the essence of the brand, what we have been calling the brand definition. Most advertising media are not particularly good at communicating complex messages or detail on product characteristics and benefits; they work best with what are called 'single-minded propositions'.

The single-minded proposition

Identify the single most motivating and differentiating thing that you can say about your brand. This will be your single-minded proposition. This is the point at which advertisers and brand managers come together – the single-minded proposition is of course the articulation through a particular medium of the brand definition. If it isn't, then you are in trouble – either your agency isn't listening, or your brand definition is incommunicable, or you are using the wrong medium.

Perhaps there is much that can be said about your brand, its definition is more complex than a simple USP (see Chapter 1), but take care not to try too much through any one advertisement. Over the course of a promotional campaign it may be possible to build up a series of individual single-minded propositions, but each specific activity within the campaign should perhaps aim to tackle just one or two at a time.

Kyocera

Kyocera, the office equipment manufacturer, recently ran a series of press adverts for its Ecosys brand of printers, with a strong central theme and a series of individual messages – one per advert. The campaign was designed to establish a clear link between Kyocera's unique capabilities (based on its technology) and a single-minded identification of the customer's needs – business efficiency and environmental concern. Each advert identified a different aspect of the technology, but used a consistent tag line throughout: 'Because business demands efficiency and the earth needs attention'.

Communicating the brand's unique signature – brand DNA

Single-minded propositions are a good start, but they still might not represent the essence of the brand. They might actually represent short-term tactics, like a 10 per cent discount at B&Q on Bank Holiday Monday, or a last chance to buy an Abbey National ISA before the end of the tax year. Useful messages, but hardly building a unique brand definition. We are perhaps still in the realms of advertising rather than brand advertising.

Brand advertising must communicate the brand definition, and it is useful here to consider an analogy introduced by Iain Ellwood: the brand definition as DNA. Like DNA, the brand definition is a unique signature that runs through every manifestation of that brand: its name, its design, its substance, its advertising – every interaction with the customer. A brand of mineral water that has *purity* as its brand definition, or DNA signature, must ensure for instance that its bottles are clean on the outside as well as the inside. However great the ad, it won't sell dirty bottles. Ellwood advises that this DNA signature must be '*as concentrated, succinct and powerful as possible so that it can survive intact as it is communicated across media types*'.

Two brands in competition may each have unique propositions, and the eventual winner may not be the one with the 'best' proposition, nor even the best short-term, single-minded propositions, but the one best able to communicate its proposition as expressed in its DNA. This is the value of good brand advertising.

Magicote

Magicote paint launched the first widely available non-drip gloss on the UK paint market and fast adopted a good single-minded proposition, 'ease of use'. It was a good proposition, for a while, but had two fatal flaws. First, it was a proposition that allowed others to catch up as they developed their own easier-to-use paints. Second, it failed to move with the times as ease of use became taken for granted and trickier and more fundamental problems were being unearthed, like, 'will those two colours match or should we just stick to magnolia?' In the battle of the paint brands it was Dulux that emerged triumphant, not because of the Old English sheepdog, but because of a more powerful brand definition, a stronger DNA. The Dulux DNA was less tangible, but far more beguiling – it was about giving people the confidence to transform their homes.

The problems with advertising...

There are several 'problems' with using advertising to build the brand definition. Often these apparent 'problems' are in fact hugely helpful, serving to test your assumptions about what your brand is and where it is headed:

■ **Advertisements must reflect the mood of the times, and that mood can change fast.** Ads can be changed in weeks or even days, but can the brands that they promote change as quickly, and still retain credibility? There is often a tension between the creative team at the advertising agency who want to make their work as up to the minute as possible, and the brand manager who must judge whether the latest developments in advertising technique or the latest 'in' terminology or symbols of street culture will actually be good for the brand's definition. The problem is a good one, continually testing the brand to check that it is relevant to its customers in substance and in spirit.
■ **Once started, you can never stop, and the road ahead keeps on growing longer.**

Club biscuits

The Club brand once 'owned' the UK market for the break-time chocolate biscuit until it chose one year to pull back on advertising and regard the money saved as extra profit. It was after all the brand leader – what harm could one year do? It was its bad luck (or was it brand myopia?) that this decision corresponded with a massive campaign behind the Penguin brand with Derek Nimmo's famous stuttering tag line. Penguin never looked back and Club never regained its position.

Branding is a long-term investment and the promotional plan for a brand must be a long-term activity. Consistency of spend is everything, hard as that might be for chief financial officers to understand.

■ **The same old adverts can wear thin after a while.** Consumers *'are like roaches – you spray them and spray them and they get immune after a while'*. David Lubars, a remarkably candid advertising executive in the Omnicom group, quoted by Naomi Klein in *No Logo*, expresses a truth that demonstrates the weakness of advertising compared to the substance of the product or the service. We get tired of adverts, or immune to their hold over us, however good they might be, but we don't get tired of a good product. It's another of those good problems, alerting us to the fact that while adverts and other promotional techniques must be recreated almost continually, genuine propositions through the product and the service can be maintained for much longer. Putting effort into maintaining and enhancing those propositions will be worth every penny.

■ **The 'production' can overpower the message.** *'Advertising at its best achieves all its commercial objectives, but also enters the popular culture,'* says Rupert Howell, Chairman of HCCL. This is a noble notion, but I suspect most clients would prefer that it was the brand that entered the popular culture, not the ad.

■ **Advertising is seen by many as intrusive.** The argument is often put that advertising provides us with choice, or is it more the perception that we are making informed choices? Knowing an ad tells us that we know something about the brand and the product. This is powerful stuff, but must be handled with care if we are to avoid the excesses of 'brand advertising fluff'.

■ **Audiences are becoming more 'literate' – they see the tricks of the trade – and in many cases more cynical.** Some brands have responded to this by lampooning themselves and their adverts. Often the adverts so produced acquire cult status (McDonald's use of the Pearl & Dean format being a case in point) but it is far from clear whether they actually build the brand's own status.

The cynical audience is sometimes handled by presenting a cynical message, or a cynical personality. Egg financial services, targeted at a younger and more cynical audience, chose to play on this by using Zoë Ball to present a cynical assessment of its approach, suggesting as she did that at least those Egg folk are like me, and so, like you. A complex but no less powerful emotional charge.

Right media, right execution

The media

If the purpose of the advertisement is to build the brand's image then it is not only the content that is important, but also the medium and the execution. As content, both of the following are fine: '*Avonlea* free-range eggs – on sale here, £2 a dozen'; '*Amy Johnson's* flying lessons – £150 an hour'. But only one of them is going to work chalked on a blackboard by the side of the road.

Each medium, from TV to press, from the internet to trade shows, has its own strengths and weaknesses as a means of building the brand. TV is good for mass awareness and communicating emotional values, but poor on detail. The internet has pretty much the reverse qualities. The right choice of media should not be a question of budget. Better not to advertise at all than to choose a cheaper but inappropriate medium. Nor do you have to go for the most expensive media, as the section on budgets (below) will show.

Placing an ad in a national newspaper is effectively associating your brand with the newspaper's brand, and all that it represents. Here's a fun exercise: try to find the same advert for something in the *Sun* and the *Guardian*...

EasyJet makes very effective use of 'buy now' ads for its low-cost European air fares. The placement in a daily paper gives the ad an immediacy and a sense of urgency, and at least in EasyJet's early days the 'association' with the big-name papers was important in helping to build credibility for a new business taking on the big boys.

The precise placement of advertisements in the chosen medium is also vital. Many brands that make use of the press will insist that their adverts are not placed next to stories of a 'depressing nature'. Still there are disasters in this regard, like the advert for slimming products that ran adjacent to a breaking story on a new and particularly dreadful famine in East Africa. Advertising on US TV news channels almost ceased in the days following the New York World Trade Center disaster.

The execution

It cannot be said too many times – this is a job for the professionals. Consider the necessary conditions for any effective communication:

- **It must reach the target audience.** How about the award-winning TV commercial for the ultimate in business-class airline seats that is put out at 3 pm on a weekday?
- **It must penetrate their attention, through a combination of timeliness, relevance and simplicity.** The TV remote control has consigned many TV ads to the 'mute' dustbin. Ads now have to be better made and more interesting than TV programmes (perhaps not so hard in these days of dumbing down, reality television, and fly-on-the-wall docu-soaps). The 'what on earth is this an advert for' technique is one angle, the running story is another – witness the Gold Blend saga of next-door neighbours or the 'Nicole?' 'Papa?' marathon for the Renault Clio.
- **It must communicate the intended message.** I once saw a press advert for cigars showing a dinner-jacketed man sitting opposite an admiring companion, the source of her admiration clearly being the cigar on which he puffed. The tag line insinuated that your choice of cigar was one of the ways that you demonstrated your concern for your loved ones. Unfortunately, this particular advert carried the government health warning noting that passive smoking can cause cancer – so much for love and attention.
- **It must *bond* the message to the brand name.** '*Beanz Meanz Heinz.*'

Beyond advertising

Telling people stuff is not enough – you want to know what they think about what you tell them, and you want to be able to influence their subsequent actions. Advertising can be a rather one-way activity; something the brand does to the customer rather than a genuine interaction.

In this sense, the B2B and service brand has something of an advantage over the FMCG brand as it finds itself interacting on a personal level with its customers. An advantage, that is, if the value of these interactions is recognised – the automated CRM (customer relationship management) or call centre approach to customer relations has a long way to go before it can compare with the direct one-to-one contact, and at its present level of sophistication can be positively damaging to a brand's image. I have ceased doing business with a famous brand (it shall remain nameless) that manages to send me a birthday card every year (the result I believe of a massive investment in a CRM system) but cannot answer its phones and, when it does, cannot proceed without some poor soul having to navigate me through endless screens of questions.

Budgets – does it all come down to money?

How much to spend – the toughest question of them all? On the one hand, we recall Henry Ford's comment on advertising expenditure, that half of the money is wasted. Unfortunately you can never be certain which half. On the other hand, we see brand plans strangled at birth by parsimonious promotional budgets.

People have tried various methods to fix on the right amount – a percentage of sales revenue, a percentage of profit, some benchmark based on competitors' spend, last year's plus or minus a percentage dreamt up by the finance department. All are used frequently, but none of them are remotely satisfactory. There is only one basis on which to determine the budget – how much is required to achieve the goals for the brand? If the money is not available, then revise your plans for the brand. None of this says that you shouldn't seek creative ways to stretch a budget.

Stretching a small budget

A small DIY brand with a budget too small for the hoped-for TV campaign launched a new product through poster sites, and moreover, they booked only a third of the sites recommended to them by the agency. The product was a fairly complex wood treatment – not an impulse buy, and one where reputation and dependability would be important. Posters were placed on the main routes to major DIY stores such that the consumer would see them just before arriving at the store. In store, the consumer was faced with a bewildering choice of options, but the last thought sown in their mind outside the store was an image of this manufacturer's product, and the association helped build a sense of credibility and trust for the brand and its new product.

Kodak

Kodak once ran a one-page ad in a leading photography magazine that consisted simply of a plain yellow page with the text – 'Our real advert is on page 5, 12, 28 and 37'. On each of these pages would be a beautiful photograph as part of an article with the reference to the film used, Kodak of course. This was a clever way to maximise impact on a slim budget with almost no production costs – usually a high part of the spend for a brand like Kodak that must always 'look its best'.

Getting your money's worth: tracking

If you do aim to spend millions on high-profile advertising, and also aim to prove Henry Ford wrong, then you must know what this spend is doing for your brand. It is vital to track the effectiveness of what will almost certainly be your biggest brand expenditure. Tracking goes beyond the impact on sales, and in any case there are often too many competing variables to be confident of pinning growth on a promotional campaign. For a £5 million TV campaign it will be worth spending the additional £80,000 to measure the campaign's impact on customer perceptions and attitudes. A typical tracking study would look at levels of awareness (often called the cut through of the medium), what perceptions are formed of the brand or product, what promises are seen to be made, what level of belief or confidence exists that they will be upheld, and what disposition does the audience have to make a purchase? Only with such information can you go to your chief financial officer with hand on heart and say that the investment in your brand really was worth making.

A recent trend in working with agencies is to pay by results. While this can work just fine for an advert intended to boost sales by the end of the quarter, will this trend threaten the longer-term development of brand definitions? If short-term measures override the long term then the answer must be yes, short-term promotional techniques will come to the fore. The brand owners must take care to choose the right measures of performance for their brand-building aspirations. The practice of ad tracking as described here can be one of the more helpful measures in this regard.

16

Briefing the agency – making sure it works for you

The huge number of agencies available to help with every conceivable aspect of branding and promotion can be rather overwhelming. To add to the problem, too many large agencies behave as if they are from a superior species compared to mere business folk. Don't ignore the smaller agencies; it is here that the real gold dust can often be found. Get them on their way up...

Prepare the brief

The agency will need to know as much about the following as you can tell it (and if it says it doesn't, then perhaps it is not the agency for you):

- the market, dynamics and trends;
- the main competitors;
- your business strategy;
- your method of market segmentation, and the target segments;
- your brand positioning strategy;
- your current brand definition;

■ your future planned brand definition;
■ your promotional plan and desired outcomes for the brand;
■ your single-minded proposition (unless you are engaging its help to determine one for you);
■ supporting evidence for this proposition;
■ the preferred media;
■ any restrictions on your ability to promote – financial, legal, moral and so on;
■ timings and budgets.

Agencies that show too much concern with the last of these points before understanding your purpose and objectives may be helping you with your selection process more than they think.

Once the brief is complete, select the agencies you wish to have a response from. Don't go for too many. First, the briefing process is time-consuming. Second, receiving the agency proposals will be even more time-consuming. Third, it is unfair on an agency to ask it to put in a significant amount of work if it is one of a large number under consideration.

Getting to the shortlist of agencies to brief will be a combination of references from colleagues, perhaps ruling out those used by the competition, and an assessment of their track record of success in similar areas. This last is not a question of 'advertising awards' and the like; rather, it is an assessment of how successful the clients of the agency have been.

Some 'rules' on briefing the agency

1. Take the time to give a full briefing.
2. Give the agency a written copy of the brief.
3. Be very clear on objectives, timings and budgets.
4. Agencies should welcome your creative thoughts, but try to leave the final creative process to the experts.
5. Ask for the agency's questions.
6. Encourage a critical assessment from the agency.
7. Give the agency as much information as possible on your selection process – timing, criteria, competitors, etc. Help it to do a good job; this is not an obstacle course you are setting it.

8. By when do you want its response, and in what format?
9. Be very clear on how you wish it to respond; is it just ideas, or do you want a full campaign proposal?

Some 'rules' on receiving an agency proposal

1. Allow it the time it requires.
2. Start by restating the objectives of the activity, or ask the agency to do so.
3. Use those objectives as your test. Try not to be swayed by the flood of exciting creative ideas; the important question is: will the ideas achieve your objective?
4. Demand full costings for any proposals.

One last thing: don't forget that the agency works for *you*.

17

The brand health check

What are the components of the ideal brand? Can there be such a thing? 'Brand leadership' was long the goal of brand managers, defined most commonly as having the biggest market share. So the ideal brand was the biggest brand. Statistics were quoted showing that in the grocery market only the largest brand made money, while third and fourth brands were fast disappearing, replaced by own labels. The syndrome has not spread, as threatened, to all markets. Now, the obsession with size has in more recent years started to evolve into an obsession with reputation.

Even those still concerned with size have moved on from simple comparisons of sales versus their nearest competitors. Rather than share of sales, they will measure '*share of voice*' – the proportion of the total communication in the sector that their brand accounts for, or '*share of mind*' – the level of recognition their brand achieves in the customer's mind.

A drinks brand might even talk of '*share of throat*', a recognition that its non-alcoholic fizzy concoction is in competition not just with other fizzy concoctions but with beer, wine, tea, coffee, milk, and even with water.

Looking beyond size, Sir Richard Branson has said that he wishes Virgin to be the most *respected*, not the *biggest* brand. Perhaps one mark of a brand leader is not its percentage of sales, or even share of voice, mind or stomach, but that everyone else wants to copy it.

It will be quite clear by now that attempting to define the ideal brand is an impossible task in anything but the most general sense. Circumstances make the individual brand what it must be, and the brand helps create the circumstances. A healthy brand is an easier test, hence the self-assessment health check that follows, shown in Table 17.1.

An additional means of assessing your current level of performance, and your progress towards branding excellence through enhanced brand management, is the Branding Performance Map® . This tool is available from INSIGHT Marketing and People; details can be found in 'Contacting the author'.

Table 17.1 The brand health check

Health Criteria The healthy brand:	Healthy	Could Be Improved	Unhealthy
is based on a proposition of genuine substance and value to the target customer			
communicates a clear and powerful brand definition			
communicates a clear 'emotional charge'			
communicates an attractive and relevant personality			
wins, builds and retains customer loyalty			
is well known by the target customer			
is held in high esteem by the target customer			
communicates and evidences a unique match between the company's capabilities and the customer's needs			
is a source of competitive advantage			
is an investment of increasing value that others will want to own			

Table 17.1 The brand health check *continued*

Health Criteria The healthy brand:	Healthy	Could Be Improved	Unhealthy
maintains its relevance over time by evolving in response to changing customer expectations and perceptions			
increases the profitability of the business			
is consistent with the business strategy			
makes sense within the business's brand architecture			
provides a protective 'halo' for growth strategies			
provides a barrier to entry for new entrants or substitutes			
is uniquely positioned in the market and creates a relevant space in the customer's mind			
communicates and demonstrates a clear sense of value			
interacts consistently with the customer on as many fronts and on as many occasions as possible			
cements the brand definition into the customer's mind through interactions and positive associations			
is managed and supported consistently over time			
has values that can be applied consistently and successfully to all parts of the marketing mix and through all promotional media			
makes people want to get their hands on it			

Contacting the author

Should you have any questions or wish to discuss any of the issues raised in this book, or perhaps would like help with developing your own brand, please feel free to contact Peter Cheverton at:

E-mail: customer.service@insight-mp.com
Tel: +44(0)1753 822990

Other titles in the Kogan Page Creating Success series

The above titles are available from all good bookshops. For further information on these and other Kogan Page titles, or to order online, visit the Kogan Page website at **www.kogan-page.co.uk**

The new *Creating Success* series

Published in association with **THE SUNDAY TIMES**

Dealing with
Difficult People

Roy Lilley

0 7494 4751 6   Paperback   2006

Develop your
NLP Skills

Andrew Bradbury

0 7494 4558 0   Paperback   2006

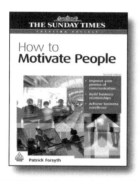

How to
Motivate People

Patrick Forsyth

0 7494 4551 3   Paperback   2006

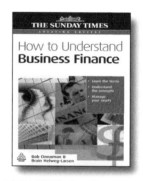

How to Understand
Business Finance

Bob Cinnamon &
Brain Helweg-Larsen

0 7494 4668 4   Paperback   2006

How to
**Write a
Business Plan**

Brian Finch

0 7494 4553 X   Paperback   2006

How to
**Write a
Marketing Plan**

John Westwood

0 7494 4554 8   Paperback   2006

For further information on how to order, please visit

www.kogan-page.co.uk

KOGAN
PAGE

The new *Creating Success* series

Published in association with **THE SUNDAY TIMES**

0 7494 4552 1   Paperback   2006

0 7494 4550 5   Paperback   2006

0 7494 4560 2   Paperback   2006

0 7494 4561 0   Paperback   2006

0 7494 4559 9   Paperback   2006

0 7494 4665 X   Paperback   2006

For further information on how to order, please visit

www.kogan-page.co.uk

KOGAN
PAGE